Comprehensive
Transport Planning

Comprehensive Transport Planning

G.R.Wells

C.Eng., M.I.C.E., F.I.H.E., F.S.S.

CHARLES GRIFFIN & COMPANY LTD
London and High Wycombe

CHARLES GRIFFIN & COMPANY LIMITED
Registered Office: 5A Crendon Street, High Wycombe HP13 6LE

First published 1975

ISBN: 0 85264 233 4

Set by E W C Wilkins Ltd London and Northampton
Printed in Great Britain by Compton Printing Limited, Aylesbury

Preface

Transport planning is an integral part of the whole process of planning and it is important that it is undertaken on a broad scale, encompassing whole areas. It is a continuing process — for nothing stands still, least of all the land uses, the facilities for movement and the travel demands that affect the transport system. There is therefore a continuing need for transport planners — to plan, to monitor the results of the plan, and then, inevitably, to replan.

Transport planning is a comprehensive process. It is not enough to consider roads or public transport alone, nor to consider an urban area in isolation from its hinterland. Transport planning must take into account the interaction of all means of movement and the effects of different levels of restraint upon the overall movement pattern. The 'best' system of overall movement has to be developed — by the comparison of alternatives, taking account of the impact on society as a whole, rather than just the advantages to the traveller.

The comprehensive approach and the broad scope of overall movement consideration involves both engineers and planners in disciplines with which they are sometimes less than familiar. The consideration of integrated movement packages necessitates the use of new appraisal techniques. This book attempts to introduce the reader to disciplines which may be new to him — the commercial approach of public transport operations, the use of parking as a restraint mechanism, the transportation study process, etc. It makes no pretence to complete coverage — several of the subjects looked at in individual chapters deserve a whole book to themselves — but it is hoped that an awareness, both of the overall picture and of the relevance of the components, will be achieved.

The book is intended to serve as a general introduction to the comprehensive transport planning process. It is hoped that it will be of assistance to practising transport engineers and planners, to those preparing for the transportation diplomas of the professional institutions, and also — by omitting the more technical inserts — to interested County Councillors and other 'laymen'.

Transport planning is a rapidly changing discipline — inevitably some part of this book will be out of date in some respect as soon as it is published. The details that do change, however, will almost certainly be developments from the foundations laid in this book. The general approach and the basic principles are unlikely to change.

Acknowledgements

I would like to acknowledge the great debt I owe to my colleagues, who have been my guides, mentors and redeemers on many occasions. They will, I am sure, understand my inability to name them all. And, I need hardly add, the views expressed in this book are not necessarily those of the Department of the Environment.

G R WELLS

1974

Contents

Glossary

Assignment: the allocation of trips with known origins and destinations to specific routes.

ATC (Area traffic control): the control of road traffic within a specified area by the linking of traffic signals, usually through a computer.

Busway: a road provided or reserved for the exclusive use of buses (differentiating between this and a bus-only lane within a road which is also open to other traffic).

Category analysis: a technique for estimating trip ends in a zone using pre-established trip rates by category of household size, composition, etc.

COBA: a computer program for the determination of an NPV/cost ratio for the economic appraisal of appropriate inter-urban road schemes.

Consumer surplus: an approach to economic evaluation used in the appraisal of urban transport strategies.

Deterrence: that which deters a traveller from making a trip — the distance to the destination, the time taken to travel, or more usually, the generalized cost of the trip.

Dial-a-Ride: a bus service within a specified area, respondent to telephone demands for collection by a flexibly-routed bus. Sometimes known as D.A.R.T. (Demand-actuated rapid transit).

Distribution, Trip: the linking of predicted trip ends, usually by gravity model.

DN ('Do-nothing'): the commonly used abbreviation (and misnomer) for the Economic Base strategy against which minimum-investment option other strategies are compared.

Generalized cost: the 'whole' cost of a journey, customarily used as the measure of spatial separation or deterrence. Takes account of the time costs, the distance costs and all terminal costs of the journey.

Generation, Trip: also known as trip-end prediction, which is almost self-explanatory — the prediction for each zone of the number of trips leaving for all destinations and the number of trips arriving from all origins.

Gravity model: the most commonly used method of trip distribution. It owes its name to the similarity of the formula (model) to Newton's concept of gravitational attraction.

Household: a separate domestic dwelling unit.

Interchange: a place where a traveller changes from one travel mode to another — ranging from a simple bus stop to a combined rail-bus station and car park.

Kiss-and-ride: the modal change whereby a traveller is driven to the station by his wife who then retains the use of the car while the husband continues his journey by rail or bus.

Link: an element in a transport network connecting two nodes.

Modal split: the division of personal trips by alternative modes — usually refers to private car : public transport.

Mode: a form of personal transport.

Node: a numbered point in a transport network defining one end of a link. Each node normally represents a significant junction or interchange but may sometimes be the location of a change in link status or a zone centroid.

NPV (Net present value): the present value of benefits over a period less the present value of the costs. The present value takes account of the earning ability of money and the earning's 'sacrificed' by delay in its receipt.

OMO: one-man-operation of buses — i.e. the driver collects fares, obviating the need for a conductor.

Optimization: the process of determining a preferred strategy by combining the better elements of a series of initial strategies while maintaining compatibility.

Park-and-ride: the change of mode whereby a traveller drives to a bus or rail station, parks his car and continues his trip by public transport.

Redistribution: the change of a trip destination, often due to a change in the spatial separation of origin and destination. It is important to recognize that a totally new trip is not involved — merely a change in destination.

Spatial separation: the distance, time or cost separating an origin from a destination. Generalized cost is the usual measure of spatial separation used in present-day transportation studies.

Strategy: an overall transport plan for an area, comprising roads, public transport services, and restraint measures as appropriate.

Traffic management: measures (usually inexpensive) for promoting the optimum use of existing facilities for the movement of people and goods by road.

Transportation study: conventionally, a package of mathematical procedures for the prediction of future travel demands and the appraisal of alternative means of coping with that demand.

Trip: in the transportation study context, a one-way movement by a person, usually assumed to be over 5 years old, from one place to another, during all or part of which journey some form of mechanically propelled transport is used.

Trip end: the start or end of a trip, in the sense that if 10 trips end at a certain location that location is said to attract 10 trip-ends. Generation (production) and attraction trip ends are linked in the transportation study process by trip distribution.

Zone: the basic unit for travel demand analysis. A basically homogeneous area of land to and from the centroid of which trips are assumed to be attracted and generated. The whole of a study area is divided into internal zones while areas outside the study area are divided into larger external zones.

1

Introducing Comprehensive Transport Planning

Every year the number of vehicles using the roads of Britain increases alarmingly. If earlier trends continue, there will be twice as many vehicles using our roads by the end of the century. Already, we are spending well over £800 000 000 a year on our roads – this figure having trebled over ten years! Yet congestion is increasing – the road network is not keeping pace with the growth of traffic. And at the same time, there is increasing public opposition to the construction of new roads – which in most cases, almost inevitably, are environmentally undesirable.

Redefining the Objective

This apparent impasse is to some extent due to a misconception of the real objective. The need is not for the provision of bigger and better roads to cope with more and more vehicles. The real objective is the MOVEMENT OF PEOPLE AND GOODS – not necessarily the movement of vehicles.

Having redefined the objective, the problem changes too. People can be moved by car or by public transport – they could even walk, but this is increasingly unlikely for other than short distances! For some movements the car is ideal, for others the bus or other mass transit mode is preferable. Comprehensive transport planning is about the optimization of the balance between the use of these modes. For inter-urban travel the flexibility of the car is a major advantage. For leisure trips in urban areas too, this flexibility is important – and the destinations of leisure, and other non-work, trips are often widely spread in both space and time, reducing their impact on congested streets. It is for the journey to work that public transport is most appropriate.

The journey from home to work occurs in a short peak period each morning and is, of course, largely repeated in reverse each evening. Many trips terminate in relatively few locations – the town centre, the industrial area, etc. As car occupancies average around 1½ persons, and buses can carry at least ten times more people per length of road-lane, a partial remedy is clear. Some trips from home to work must be attracted, or diverted, to public transport.

The 'Carrot' and the 'Stick'

Bus travel, however, is not popular with commuters, because services are too often unreliable, slow, uncomfortable and crowded, whereas a car is at least thought to be convenient and reliable. The change of mode must therefore be *induced*. This requires the use of both 'the carrot' and 'the stick'.

First, 'the carrot' — bus services must be improved, in reliability, in frequency and in convenience (and perhaps, although this is of less importance than is sometimes thought — in cost). Bus priority measures of one form or another can usually do a lot to meet these requirements. But the carrot alone is not enough, the car will still be preferred, so 'the stick' — restraint measures — must be applied. This means making the use of the car less attractive, by providing fewer parking spaces at higher cost (or better, not opening the car parks until after the commuter is at work!), by closing streets to cars, or just by allowing congestion to take effect. (This latter approach is not to be preferred as it bites indiscriminately on all road users, buses included.) Perhaps even, at some later date, differential road-use pricing or supplementary licensing could be applied, although there are operational problems in both cases.

The movement of goods in urban areas however is not something which can readily be transferred to other transport modes. The lorry is here to stay. But the 'juggernauts' engender much of the emotional outcry in many areas, most notably in residential streets in towns and small villages on through-routes. Here, palliatory measures may be appropriate — directing large lorries onto certain preferred routes, providing lorry parks in non-residential areas, or even perhaps, providing 'trans-shipment' depots outside town areas.

However, no matter what is done to induce people to change their travel mode, or goods vehicles to change their routes, there will eventually still be congestion on many roads. Before new roads are built, it is plain that the existing road system should be used as fully as possible. And this means, among other things, using roads for movement instead of for parking. Other typical traffic-management measures to improve on the use of existing roads, to move people rather than vehicles, might include some or all of the following:

    pedestrianization of central shopping-area roads
    bus priority measures — bus-only lanes etc.
    one-way systems
    linked traffic signals
    right-turn bans
    peak-hour urban clearways.

After consideration of all of these however, and the application of appropriate measures — which form the basis of the relatively short-term management aspects of urban planning — there will still be a need for some new roads. And these have to be planned.

Comprehensive Planning

Transport planning for a county — not just town or rural area in isolation, but both together — must be comprehensive, and based on financial realism (there is NEVER *enough* money). The roles of public transport, private car restraint, traffic management measures, and new road construction need to be fully integrated — both with each other and between urban and rural areas — to derive the best use of the inevitably limited resources. A transport plan is developed as a complete package of projects and policies, conceived as a unified whole. It should be implemented comprehensively in across-the-board stages in accordance with a carefully conceived, financially realistic, annual programme, derived in turn from a longer programme.

Outside the urban areas, less important inter-urban and other rural roads are often planned on the basis of simple growth factors — present-day vehicular traffic merely 'writ large' and reassigned to take advantage of new routes. Major road proposals — new motorways and the like — are usually determined on a more sophisticated basis, at national level. Their implementation however often leads to local requirements on the surrounding road network. These however are readily determined. Rural public transport services are usually determined on a social and/or requirement basis, rather than on economic or commercial criteria. Virtually all inter-urban transport planning, at other than national or regional level, is less of a problem than urban planning.

The Transportation Study

In larger urban areas, the medium-term planning of future transport systems is usually based on a transportation study — sometimes called a land-use transportation study because of its fundamental reliance on the relationships between land use and travel demand. (The medium-term-oriented transportation study is customarily developed on the basis of a single future land-use forecast. It is generally accepted that there is little traffic-significant scope for variation in such a forecast *within such a time scale*.) A transportation study is basically a computer-dependent mathematical process, founded on present-day observation, whereby future travel patterns can be predicted. In essence, the transportation study process consists of:
a) surveying the present-day travel habits of people living and/or working in the specified area,
b) developing mathematical formulae which, given details of household structure, income, car ownership, etc. in the study area, can reproduce present-day travel patterns as surveyed. The formulae (or 'models') in their simplest form are basically:
   i) trip-end prediction — determining how many trips leave a zone
                 e.g. a group of households,
   ii) trip distribution — determining the destination of these trips,
   iii) modal split — determining the mode of travel — car or bus,
   iv) assignment — determining the actual roads used,
c) using these formulae, together with predicted values for future population, incomes, etc. to predict future travel patterns,
d) comparing the merits of alternative transport systems to accommodate the predicted movements. (The comparison is on economic, operational and environmental grounds, but the final decision is inevitably a subjective one, a political decision, taking account of public opinion etc. and the relative importance of the evaluated criteria)

The Planning Process

The techniques of comprehensive transport planning aside, the *process* is similar in both urban and rural contexts. Firstly, the present transportation situation is assessed, together with financial and existing policy constraints on possible future action. Resulting from that review it is often possible to identify future problems — although this will usually require further investigation. It is important in fact to determine whether there are, or are likely to be, any problems at all! There is always a possibility that the best thing to do is . . . nothing.

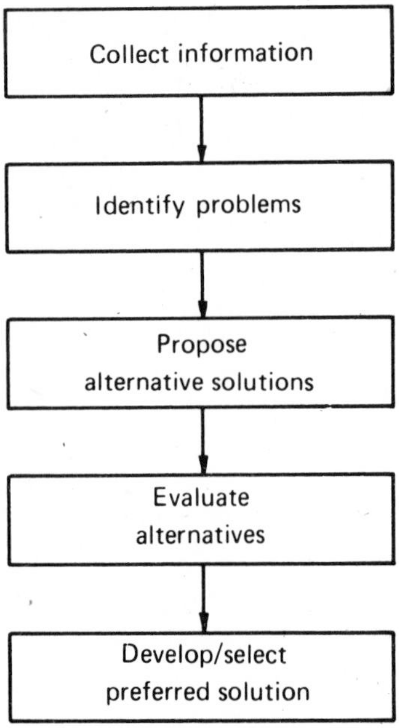

Fig. 1.1 The basic principles of the planning process

```
┌─────────────────────────┐
│   Collect information    │
└─────────────────────────┘
             │
             ▼
┌─────────────────────────┐
│    Identify problems     │
└─────────────────────────┘
             │
             ▼
┌─────────────────────────┐
│        Propose           │
│  alternative solutions   │
└─────────────────────────┘
             │
             ▼
┌─────────────────────────┐
│       Evaluate           │
│      alternatives        │
└─────────────────────────┘
             │
             ▼
┌─────────────────────────┐
│    Develop/select        │
│   preferred solution     │
└─────────────────────────┘
```

Accepting that there are problems however, we can consider the time-scale of their solution. Some problems can be solved by short-term, immediate-action measures. Others may require more detailed planning and more expenditure. In these instances stop-gap measures may be appropriate to prevent continued deterioration. In all instances it is then necessary to collect information on present-day conditions, and from that base develop a prediction of the future.

Future conditions predicted, and the problems reviewed and reconsidered, it is important to develop alternative possible solutions. The only way to determine a sensible solution is to evaluate and assess several viable possibilities and from that consideration, develop an optimum solution (to assume that there is only one solution and merely to 'test' that, is naively over-confident and virtually useless). And it must always be remembered that the solutions are comprehensive and integrated 'packages' — it may not be sensible or even possible to adopt part of one packaged solution and hope to apply it in association with part or all of another package. Any such attempted optimization needs to be re-assessed as a whole.

Transport planning is a field of considerable public interest and concern — and rightly so, for it is public money which is involved. Final decisions on transport planning are therefore not for the planner, but for the politician with his feel for public acceptability. The role of comprehensive transport planning is to provide the decision-maker with the best possible, largely quantified, advice.

Finally, transport planning is not a finite exercise. Planning decisions for the next few years may be irreversible (the new road may be under construction) but those for the medium-term may provide scope for reconsideration. It is not impossible for a whole medium-term transport plan to be abandoned in mid-stream and the planning exercise wholly redone — the effect would be that any work already started would become a commitment in the new plan. Transport planning is a continuous process — it needs continuous attention.

SUMMARY

a) The objective of comprehensive transport planning is the optimum movement of people and goods.

b) Particularly for the journey to work, public transport could be more efficient than the private car — but is less attractive.

c) To induce greater use of public transport the system needs to be improved and restraint applied to the use of the private car.

d) County transport planning should be done on a comprehensive basis, developing integrated packages of public transport, private car restraint, and the optimum use of both existing and new roads.

e) In larger urban areas, transport planning is usually based on a transportation study — a means of predicting future travel movements.

f) The preferred strategy, which is not just a collection of unrelated schemes, is best developed by optimization from a range of integrated possible packages.

g) The final choice of strategy is a political matter.

2

Strategy Development

There are many possible methods of developing an overall county strategy, and of dividing up the financial resources between different strategy components. In this chapter, one possible method is expounded — not because it is the best — but because it demonstrates the type of thinking that should be employed on this work. There will be other, perhaps better methods. They will have to incorporate the same components; they will have to make similar allowances. The important concept is to THINK INTEGRATED.

Before looking in detail at the problems of comprehensive transport planning on a county scale, let us be clear what the objective is. What are we aiming to do? The intention is to provide a comprehensive plan for the provision and integration of transportation facilities over a whole county, taking full account of the effects of such outside influences as national policies, proposed new motorways, railways, etc. Wherever possible, alternative plans or strategies are considered, in order to determine the optimum solution.

To find a solution — or develop a plan — we must first define the problem. What is wrong with the transportation facilities at present available? How far will they fall short of adequacy in the years to come? To define a problem the basic requirement is for information — information on present travel movements and on present facilities for meeting the demand for travel. And because travel demands are a function of the land use, information is also required on future development proposals (a new town or housing estate, or the opening of a new industrial complex or port facility, will generate increased travel demands).

For the county as a whole — as opposed to the larger urban areas, which are dealt with in detail elsewhere in this book — the basic surveys are of course the traffic flows on the roads, the capacities and general characteristics of the roads themselves, and the demand for and supply of public transport services. This amount of data could well prove indigestible for many counties if every road were looked at, so, at least in respect of the road traffic flows, some sort of hierarchical structure needs to be imposed on the road network. Generally (and there will of course be exceptions, which for that reason alone, will be extremely important), the most important roads in the county after the national motorways and trunk roads will be those classified as 'principal' roads. Clearly though, there will be other roads of only slightly less importance, which should also be investigated.

Future Prediction

Knowing then the present-day traffic flows on the more important non-urban roads in the county, these can be projected into the future. How, and how far? Tackling the first question first, consider the projection of the traffic patterns forward in time. It is acknowledged that the travel demand between two centres of population is a function of the product of the two populations and an inverse function of their spatial separation. Thus:

$$T_{ij} = K P_i P_j F (S_{ij})$$

or possibly

$$T_{ij} = K P_i P_j / S_{ij}^n$$

where

T_{ij} = trips from town i to town j

P_i, P_j = population of towns i and j

S_{ij} = some measure of the spatial separation of towns i

and j

F = some function of S

K = a constant

n = a power, varying around 2.0 (say between 1 and 2.5)

Inter-urban travel is unlikely to undergo significant redistribution, because most urban centres of population are already established and therefore likely to change relatively little over a planning period (as compared to the establishment of a new town on a 'green fields' site) and also because of the relatively small change likely in the spatial separation (a function of longer distances than urban movement).

Of greater importance in predicting the future level of inter-urban traffic is the change in real income and the effect that this has on vehicle ownership. Subject then to manual adjustments to allow for significant changes in land use, inter-urban traffic may adequately be projected into the future by the use of the 'Tanner factors'. Derived from the TRRL Report LR 543 these allow, with interpolation, the general traffic level to be projected from any year to any other, within the period 1971 to 2010. The relevant index figures, which are quoted below, are readily converted into factors. Thus, to predict 1991 traffic flows, in vehicles, 1975 survey data should be multiplied by a factor of 388/258 = 1.51, say 1.5.

The possibility of manual adjustment of growth-factor-projected flows was mentioned above and would be appropriate in, for example, the development of a new port complex or major hypermarket. An adequate assessment can be made of the traffic actually generated by the new facility in a specific future year and this figure can be added to the grossed-up flows on appropriate adjacent roads.

The relative importance of redistribution in inter-urban flows

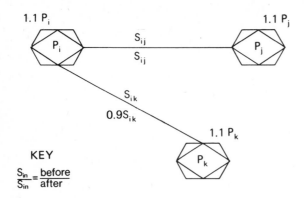

KEY

$$\frac{S_{in}}{S_{in}} = \frac{before}{after}$$

The relevance of redistribution in inter-urban movements

Consider a village with population P_i which is equidistant from 2 towns of similar size, P_j and P_k. The distances between the village and the two towns are respectively S_{ij} and S_{ik}. At present, the traffic from the village is divided equally between the two towns. Thus:

$$T_{ij} = \frac{K\,P_i\,P_j}{S_{ij}^2} = T_{ik} = \frac{K\,P_i\,P_k}{S_{ik}^2} \qquad \text{i.e. a 50/50 split.}$$

If now the population of the village and each town increases by a common 10% but the spatial separation S_{ik} is reduced by a relatively large 10%,[*] then, where T'_{ij}, T'_{ik} = new traffic flows:

$$T'_{ij} = \frac{1.2\,K\,P_i\,P_j}{S_{ij}^2} = 1.2\,T_{ij}$$

and

$$T'_{ik} = \frac{1.2\,K\,P_i\,P_k}{(0.9\,S_{ik})^2} = 1.5\,T_{ik} = 1.5\,T_{ij}$$

i.e. a 56/44 split;

thus, if redistribution were to be ignored, the error would be 12%, which is within the limits of predictive error in this sort of exercise.

---

[*] Consider a typical inter-urban journey, from village to town, of say 25 kilometres. A 5 km stretch of the road is in need of improvement. The overall journey speed is 50 km/h based on journey times of 8 minutes for the poor 5 km stretch, and 22 minutes for the remainder of the trip. If the poor section is improved, it will enable a speed of perhaps 60 km/h to be attained, or a section time of 5 minutes. This means that the overall time for the 25 km trip is now 27 minutes, a saving of 10%.

Tanner factor indices

Year	Vehicle Index	Pcu index*
1971	220	267
1975	258	304
1980	307	356
1985	346	397
1990	383	438
1995	410	469
2000	435	498
2005	458	527
2010	478	551

* Note — pcu = passenger car units, a measure of traffic flow wherein, in this case, public service and heavy goods vehicles are classified as equivalent to three passenger cars or light goods vehicles. Pcu indices are provided for completeness, although in an exercise of this nature there is no need for this — probably spurious — accuracy.

The Design Year

The determination of how far into the future a comprehensive transportation plan should be looking is influenced by the sequence of national census years. Because of the importance of census data in both land-use forecasting and also as back-up information in urban transportation studies, most transportation planning is geared to the 5-year-interval series — 1971, 1976, 1981, 1986, 1991, 1996 . . .

Because most road schemes and many public transport or parking infrastructure proposals take several years from conception to completed construction, and also because the whole planning process is a time-consuming one, it is unlikely that any decisions can be implemented in the first three to five years from the start of planning. Again, because the planning process is involved and not inexpensive, the longer one can sensibly look ahead, the better. But to predict future land uses more than 10 to 15 years ahead is unrealistic — and indeed, although 10 years of future development may to a large extent be committed, 15 years ahead is stretching such prediction to the limit. It is, in fact, only acceptable to estimate that far ahead because land-use changes have to be very large and unexpected before they cause major transportation planning differences.

In any case, planning is not a once-and-for-all-time exercise, but a continuing process. Within a few years the whole process will need to be reviewed, the prediction date moved forward and early plans subjected to re-evaluation. In this re-examination process the land-use assumptions made originally can be checked and amended if necessary.

For all the reasons mentioned above, a transportation plan is usually geared to a census year about 13 to 17 years ahead, in other words, spanning about the 15-year ideal. The 15-year ideal period can then be broken down into:

Years 0 to 5 — Plans already in hand being implemented. Little new planning possible; only the completion of commitments and some traffic-management measures.

Years 5 to 10 — The first phase of the new plan. This phase is unlikely to be further amended, it will become the 'commitments' of the next plan revision.

Years 10 to 15 — The second phase of the new plan. This part of the plan is subject to checking and possible amendment in the plan revision cycle, particularly if there are significant changes in the original land-use predictions. Effectively, the first phase of the second plan.

The Link with Structure Planning

It is important to bear in mind that the 15-year plan just described is not a plan conceived or adopted in isolation. As has been stated earlier, planning is a continuing discipline — the 15-year transport plan must fit into the larger framework of an overall, longer-term plan — a Structure Plan.

A structure plan is intended to be basically a non-specific documentation of intended policies; a diagrammatic-plan-in-words; a broadbrush concept of a county at about the end of the century (following the census-year series as before, this is often taken as 2001). And transportation policies need to be considered, not only as one facet, albeit important, of a long-term structure plan, but also in the context of a middle-term, more detailed structure plan action programme of specific policies and schemes.

Because the end-date of a structure plan is so remote (and in fact the very term end-date is erroneous in its conflict with the desirable non-specificity) it is better to plan forward towards it, rather than back from it. This is particularly important in the capital-intensive transportation field, where a scheme or policy implemented too early is costing more money than it need (taking a logical, cash-discounted view).

So a, say, 1991* comprehensive transport plan is developed first, based on a single, most-likely, land-use prediction. From that middle-term fix it is possible for a structure plan to look further into the increasingly murky future, taking account of the alternative land-use dispositions and considering the 2001 transportation strategies allied to each of these options. However, given a fixed total amount of transportation finances, it is likely that, from any one 1991 fix, a suitable transport plan could be developed to fit almost any 2001 land-use disposition, with virtually equal merit. Structure plans, at the turn of the century, are likely to be dependent on matters other than transportation for the selection of the optimum land use.

Having set the comprehensive transport planning process in its place in the context of overall county-wide structure planning, it is now appropriate to look more closely at the narrower field of transportation. To reiterate, the aim is to produce a county-wide integrated plan for the movement of people and goods for a design-year about 13 to 17 years ahead — in this case, 1991. And the plan will be based on a single prediction of land-use disposition at that end-date.

We have decided that before the problems of county movement can be assessed, surveys of present facilities are necessary and, at least in the case of inter-urban highway conditions, the flows can be projected forward by adjusted factoring. From this exercise at least the major bottlenecks can be identified — and in any case, an assessment-of-need exercise can be undertaken. This will be explained briefly later, but for a detailed exposition, the reader is referred to the author's earlier book *Highway Planning Techniques*.

* Henceforth, in this book, the design date for transportation planning will be assumed to be 1991 — to avoid repeated explanations and/or confusion.

Strategy Components

Before the question of developing a strategy for the county is further considered, it is relevant to review the components of county-wide transport planning which, even in this limited context, ignoring air, sea and pipe transport, are legion. A list of transport strategy components (which must vary from county to county) in random order of importance, and not necessarily comprehensive, includes:

a)   inter-urban trunk roads and motorways — by definition, those significant at national level,

b)   inter-urban county roads — principal roads,

c)   inter-urban county roads — lesser roads,

d)   county bus services — at village level,

e)   county bus services — the county-wide route network,

f)   county bus services — bus services *in* smaller towns,*

g)   urban roads in smaller towns,*

h)   parking policies in smaller towns,*

i)   urban roads in larger towns,*

j)   public transport services in larger towns,*

k)   parking policy in larger towns,*

l)   total level of finance over plan period for whole county,

m)   financial split — urban/rural,

n)   financial split — between different towns.

* For the sake of clarity, smaller/ larger towns could in this context be considered as those with populations of less or more than, say, 100 000, *but*, this split is extremely subjective and must depend on the towns concerned.

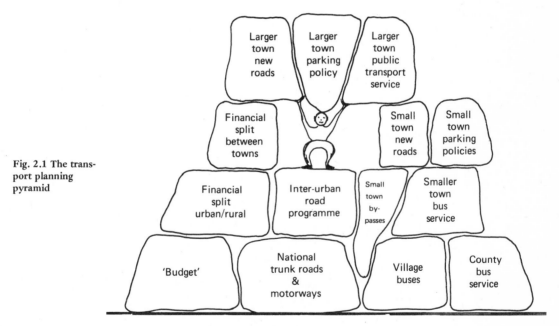

Fig. 2.1 The transport planning pyramid

Clearly the problem of building an integrated plan from that list of components is very considerable. The comprehensive transport planner is somewhat like a juggler with umpteen miscellaneous items in the air, who wants to build them into a stable pyramid. His best plan must therefore be to remove from mid-air the easiest or most stable items first, leaving the more difficult items to be precariously balanced atop the then more stable pile. Translating that somewhat mixed metaphor into practical transport planning terms, we firm-up first on the more readily determined components before proceeding to develop strategic plans involving the more nebulous and integrated components.

The Financial Constraint

In the county context, as opposed to national planning, the network of inter-urban trunk roads and motorways is predetermined, and — equally important — is not a financial charge on a county transport plan. It is therefore a prime contender among the components for predetermination. Having fixed the easiest component, it is probably desirable next to lay the important foundation stone of the level of funds available over the plan period. Despite what anyone may rashly and unthinkingly suggest, be he engineer, planner or politician, money does *not* grow on trees! Transport planners are involved in the planning of the use of public money, which derives in large part from rates and taxes levied on the public. Obviously, no one wants to pay more taxes than are necessary, so public money is always short, and certainly finite. If there were unlimited public funds, transport planning might be easy — but this is not the case, so transportation planners need a realistic approach to financial limitations.

It is necessary then for a transport planner and/or his financial colleagues to take a view on the amount of finance likely to be available for all aspects of transportation in the county within the plan period. It may be that a suitable basis for planning can be obtained from central government. In the past, the Department of the Environment has given advice on transportation expenditure planning assumptions — but usually only for specific urban areas and then only in the context of transportation studies with which they were associated. The DOE's advice has historically been based on a long-range view of the future national availability of transportation funds, this national 'cake' being cut up on the basis of urban population together with certain other unspecified considerations. But this advice has even then, in the past, only usually been available in respect of urban finances — excluding any rural or inter-urban availability of funds.

Without the restricted benefit of an earlier DOE advice of possible future urban funds, and even with it, to allow for other areas, a county transport planner will probably wish to take his own view of overall long-range county-wide transportation finances. This need not be such an awesome prospect as it may first appear however.

Every county will have records of capital expenditure on principal and other county roads, plus any other transportation items, such as car parks etc. over past years. It is probably not difficult to extract those items of capital expenditure in terms of roads in towns and roads outside towns — urban and rural expenditure. As long as the expenditure figures are related to, say, a ten-year period in the recent past, and discounted to account for inflationary trends, they should be useful as a guide to the necessary long-range view. Because we are dealing with transportation as an integrated whole, any public transport subsidies or purchases of new stock by or for a local public transport undertaking would also be taken into account.

Even though a sizeable part of every county's transportation expenditure will perhaps be derived, directly or indirectly, from central government, some part of it will inevitably need to be found from the county's ratepayers. And sudden major fluctuations in the rates are frowned upon by Councillors, Treasurers and ratepayers alike. It is not an unrealistic initial approach therefore to consider the past level of county transportation expenditure (both roadwork capital expenditure and expenditure on public transport stock and subsidies) and to continue this forward as an indication of expenditure per year, in base-year prices, i.e. excluding future inflationary trends, over the new plan period. These annual figures, summed over the plan period should represent the basis — initially, at any rate — for determining the transportation expenditure planning assumption — the 'budget'.

It is absolutely essential at this stage to understand that no financial commitments are being made — major assumptions are no doubt being made, but only to ensure planning realism. Therefore, and also because we are planning rather than accounting, any expenditure figure derived as above — or by any other equally realistic approach — should be rounded off, certainly to the nearest £5 million, and possibly to £10 million in a large county.

It will be argued that county transport planning policies may change markedly during or between plans. It is unlikely however that the overall, say 15-year, level of expenditure will change by a significant percentage, certainly during the perhaps 5 years between major plan reviews. It may also be argued that one of the reasons for county-wide transport planning is to obtain grants of funds from central government, therefore the larger the amount asked for, the more likelihood of getting what is *really* wanted. This approach, however, somewhat naively assumes that central government will not have taken an independent broad-brush view of the appropriate level of long-range planning funds for individual counties. In any case, to base a comprehensive integrated plan on an unrealistically high-expenditure assumption, which is not capable of being achieved is patently not planning, but mere horse-trading!

A further point in favour of realistic financial forecasting is the inevitable increases in cost of most transport items — not due to inflation, but to improved designs or earlier under-estimating. The case must always come back to the point that some sizeable part of all transport expenditure has to be met from the county's own resources — the rates. Over-optimistic and expensive planning due to lack of realism can only lead to delays in the implementation of schemes and policies while plans are recast and re-assessed, and to the inevitable associated political embarrassment.

Rural Public Transport

So, a financial limit, however broad and subject to later adjustment, having been fixed, we can move forward to determine other fixes in the county transportation plan. An element which lends itself to political decision-making, on largely emotive/subjective lines, and is also at the moment less amenable to objective analysis, is the policy for the level of public transport service in rural and inter-urban parts of the county. It should be borne in mind that even in the late 1980s and early 1990s there will still be many people without their own motorcars — who will still be at too low an income level to afford a car. These people, with the wives of car-using, one-car-owning husbands — and it has been suggested that altogether they will represent as much as 50 per cent of the population — will continue to rely on public transport. This is a fact of life and decisions on rural public transport will of necessity have to take cognizance of this requirement.

On a nation-wide basis, public transport services are declining. It is therefore likely that in most county rural areas the same trend is mirrored. If left unchecked, to operate from a purely commercial standpoint, rural services could well deteriorate over a plan period to about 30 per cent of their present-day level. From a social service viewpoint therefore, if some public transport service is to be retained in rural areas, then a subsidy will be required.

The political decision might sensibly be along the lines of: 'All centres of population of x thousand or more should be provided with a reliable public transport service to the nearest town/shopping centre (or to the regional centre) at not less frequently than y times per day/week.' Given this sort of commitment it is not an insuperable task to calculate the total cost, over the plan period, of the annual subsidy entailed in ensuring this level of service. And from this commitment, the general level of the county bus service is established, together with the essential capital commitment to revenue support — subsidy.

There still remains the question of public transport services to the more remote villages which fall outside the policy detailed above. Once again, it must be a political decision whether to provide them with a public transport service or not. It is in these circumstances that the provision of village buses as described in Chapter 3 is worthy of consideration.

But it would, of course, be wrong to investigate only that solution — perhaps the alternative of a once-or-twice-a-week regular bus service or a 'post-bus' service might afford an adequate and/or politically more acceptable service. It is even, on occasions, suggested that individual motor-scooters might be presented to village inhabitants to provide a cheaper transport facility than an uneconomic bus service. The choice is likely to be largely subjective and therefore appropriately political, and therefore a matter for the transportation planner merely to tender advice on.

Once this decision has been made however — and costed in terms of commitment against the plan-period financial provision — it can form a further foundation stone in the necessary pyramid of planning policies.

Sectoral Financial Apportionment

Yet another financial foundation stone needs to be considered next. Having already determined the overall county-wide budget for the plan period, it is useful to divide this, again very broadly, into funds for urban transportation and funds for rural or inter-urban transportation. At this stage of the exercise, an initial view can perhaps best be taken on the basis of the respective populations. Thus in a county with a population of half a million, containing a large town of 200 000 inhabitants and two others of 60 000 and 40 000 each, the total budget might be divided initially into 60 per cent for the specified urban areas and 40 per cent for inter-urban and smaller urban requirements. This rough apportionment can be checked against previous years' urban/rural expenditure and if necessary or politically desirable, adjusted to more closely approach past levels.

Generally speaking this broad split of funds should be adhered to in the early planning stages. As the county plan develops, a closer look can be taken at marginal urban and inter-urban proposals, with a view to varying the apportionment.

The same principle might also reasonably be adopted for the initial financial apportionment between individual towns. The large town mentioned earlier would therefore be allotted something like two-thirds of the urban budget with the other towns planning on 20 and 13 per cent respectively. Once again, this allocation of funds can be compared with previous years' expenditures and, if necessary, adjusted accordingly.

A further ground for adjustment of the inter-town apportionment, and to some extent the urban/rural split too, is the importance attached to the large town as a regional centre. Should this consideration be a major one then the allocation of transportation funds might well be varied to ensure the town's continuing regional viability, but always within the overall total budget.

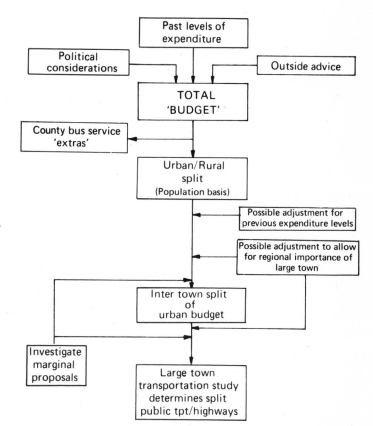

Fig. 2.2 The financial backbone of an integrated county transport plan.

The Inter-urban Programme

Earlier in this chapter we have already suggested that an Assessment-of-Need exercise should be carried out in respect of the county's inter-urban road network, on a hierarchical basis. Resulting from that exercise a list of inter-urban road schemes — including bypasses of small towns and villages — can be produced, in rough order of need. Having determined a broad level of available inter-urban finance, it is at this stage appropriate to tailor the ranked list of schemes to about one-and-a-half times the available financial budget. This provides leeway for detailed scheme consideration, which must of course include refinement of the very rough cost estimates used in the Assessment-of-Need exercise.

For initial sifting of these ranked schemes the first year economic rate-of-return method, applied to a selection of alternative solutions for each necessary improvement, is perfectly adequate. Again, the reader is referred to the author's earlier *Highway Planning Techniques*. At this stage the list of schemes could well be reduced to only ten per cent above the budget. For more detailed scheme investigation of preferred schemes, the more sophisticated NPV approach of the DOE's COBA program is recommended.

Of course, the economic assessment will not be the sole or even the major criterion in scheme selection — other matters including the potential effect on the environment will inevitably be considered, and increasingly so. At this stage too the concept of lorry routes — preferred routes for heavy vehicles, juggernauts — should be taken into account, weighting the selection of some inter-urban schemes by their preferred use in this context.

Let us now suppose that either or both the first-year economic appraisal and the COBA assessment, together with the other more subjective criteria, show a number of schemes with a significantly higher (and, by implication, acceptable) benefit than their fellows. This points to a natural limit to a programme. Should the schemes ranked above this natural break utilize *less* than the available funds previously determined so arbitrarily, this argues for a revision in the urban/inter-urban apportionment. Should the natural break occur however at a point on the ranked list where a running total of scheme costs *just* exceeds the budget, then conversely there is a case for examining the marginal urban schemes for a possible urban to rural transfer — but not for the virtually automatic adjustment of the split which a lower-level requirement might indicate. However it is much more likely that far too many apparently worthwhile schemes will be shown up by the detailed investigations. In this case, the only adjustment which should be made to the financial apportionment is basically a political one concerning the odd marginal scheme.

There is one possible exception to the principles recommended above, and that is the bypass of a small town. A bypass will, on occasions, afford considerable *urban* relief to a small town (although seldom to a large town) and where this relief can be clearly demonstrated (not just by an inter-urban scheme assessment) it is not unreasonable to use urban-allocated funds to meet the cost. It is this type of scheme which is often the correct answer to the juggernaut problem, and the effect of the juggernauts on the small-town

environment should always be a major criterion in the urban evaluation
of such a bypass.

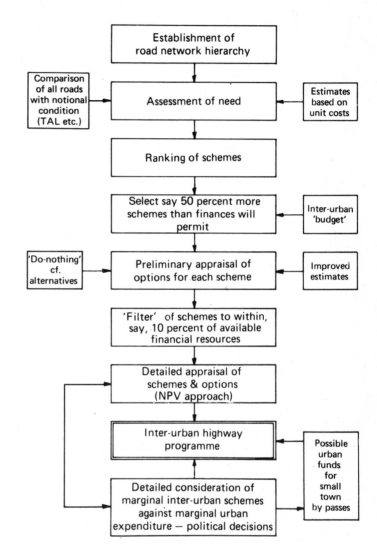

**Fig. 2.3 The inter-urban scheme
selection process**

Smaller Towns

As we move from the inter-urban aspects of a county plan towards
the increasingly urban areas, the integrated approach to transport
planning becomes more and more important. It was not unreasonable
in the inter-urban deliberations to ignore the effect of public transport
services and parking restraints, neither of which have any great
influence on inter-urban travel demands. In even a small town of, say,
30 000 population however, all the aspects of transportation need to be
considered. A town of this size does not usually, though there are
exceptions, warrant the effort and expense of carrying out a full
transportation study of the type described briefly in the first chapter
and to be considered more fully later. Notwithstanding this, many of the

processes inherent in a normal full transportation study are appropriate to the small town.

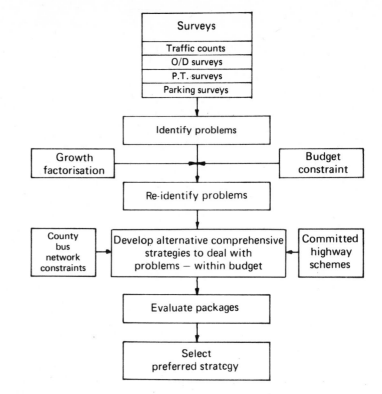

Fig. 2.4 The Planning process for smaller towns

As always, the initial requirement is for information — which means surveys. The small town can be divided into a relatively small number of traffic zones (a possible maximum of say 20 within the study area) and roadside interviews undertaken at cordon and screen-line crossing points, to determine basic peak hour and/or 24-hour origin and destination information. Alongside this survey, traffic counts for calibration purposes, public transport passenger surveys (probably on a handed-out postcard basis) and a detailed road network and parking-space inventory would be the minimum requirement. From this basic survey information, the trouble spots can be located and the major transport problems identified.

From the same data, matrices of present-day origin and destination travel demands can be built up and these in turn can then be factored, using the Furness iterative technique, which is more fully described later, to predict design year (1991) travel demands. Once the design year travel patterns are predicted, the problem areas and trouble spots of the present-day transport system should again be checked, to ensure that they are still in fact problems, and that more have not developed. This process entails building what is known as the 'Economic Base' or 'Do-Nothing' system for the design year — loading the future travel demands onto the present-day transportation system amended only by inescapable commitments (for the construction of new car parks, road improvements, etc.).

The Economic Base system — often abbreviated to DN (for 'Do-Nothing', although really meaning 'Do-Minimum') — is the basis of all comparative assessments of alternative strategies in transportation planning. Inevitably, the building of alternative strategies for testing consists of the DN plus a number of others. The testing process compares the benefits of 'Doing-something' over and above the option of Doing-nothing. Clearly then, the definition of which highway schemes and/or car parking provisions are to be taken as inescapably committed is of paramount importance — it is also a matter of applying a certain amount of political judgement.

In building alternative strategies for smaller towns, the available public transport service is seldom amenable to the sort of major changes appropriate to the larger towns. Several of the bus services operating in the town will undoubtedly be through services, planned on a county-wide basis to meet county requirements rather than those of an individual town *en route*. These services are not able to be greatly influenced on a smaller town basis. If however, there are existing or future possibilities of purely local services, the need for these should be considered in the smaller town context. And one of the most important and worthwhile of small-town bus improvements that can readily be implemented is increased penetration into housing areas.

However, in a small town there is generally neither a great need nor the possibility to divert travel from the private car to public transport. Instead, there is a need to move parking facilities off the main traffic-significant routes, into off-street car parks, to relieve shopping streets and residential areas of through traffic by traffic management measures and/or by providing relief roads, and generally to improve the urban environment — for example by designating pedestrian-only central areas.

It is important always to remember however, that there is not just one solution. The available funds will never allow the perfect solution — which it assuredly would not be — so the solution will need to be the best that can be tailored to the funds available. And the way to determine, as far as possible, the best solution is to compare several alternatives. So, against the base of the DN system, it is perhaps appropriate to compare, say, a system of various traffic management measures allied with unrenumerative (? free) but capital-intensive parking provision, perhaps, against the provision of a short but expensive inner relief road and a policy of retaining certain on-street parking facilities.

An assessment of the overall value of each small-town alternative strategy is made using appropriate operational, economic and environmental criteria as later described, and the preferred strategy is determined. The final agreement to, or amendment of this preferred strategy must, of course, like all other aspects of county transportation planning, be a political decision.

The Larger Town

Many of the components in our planning pyramid are now in place, leaving only the inter-related public transport services, parking policies and new roads in the larger town still 'in the air', to be finalized and balanced atop the pyramid. It is here that the conventional or formal transportation study is usually necessary. Although the process is inevitably more sophisticated, it is not markedly dissimilar in principle to that already described for the smaller town.

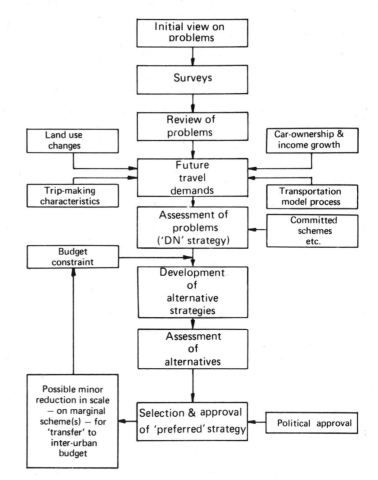

Fig. 2.5 The planning process for a larger town

As in the smaller town, surveys are undertaken and the problems shown up thereby are identified. It is in the method of predicting future demands that the major sophistication is found — future travel demands being derived from consideration of the predicted future land uses, income distribution, car ownership and population. The detailed techniques, which were mentioned in Chapter 1, are described more fully in a later chapter. Once the future travel demands are predicted, the process parallels that described for the smaller town. The development of alternative strategies is inevitably more complex however, as public transport operations and requirements need to be considered in detail, together with parking restraint policies and both immediate and long-term applications of traffic management measures.

Despite the increased sophistication of the strategies and the techniques involved, a preferred strategy is determined and again agreed by the elected county councillors. There remains one further consideration to be dealt with before finalizing the whole strategy — the possibility of marginal financial transfers back from the urban budget to the inter-urban one, or vice versa. As before, there must be a political decision on this matter, based on advice on relative operational, economic, environmental etc. merits of the schemes/policies involved. Clearly this sort of final adjustment is best kept to a minimum as far as possible.

Finally: the whole county-wide package as now assembled should be reviewed as an integrated entity, to ensure that no odd ends are left untied, and to ensure that political and operational uniformity has been maintained.

SUMMARY

a) The basic approach to county transportation planning should be to first determine the fixes, followed by those components most readily fixed politically or technically.

b) The financial constraint, which is essential for realistic planning, should be determined on a logical basis, and not with a view to horse-trading — getting as much as possible.

c) The budget is not a final constraint — merely an aid to planning.

d) Inter-urban planning should be based on a hierarchical road structure, investigated, via an assessment-of-need exercise, by individual scheme assessment and a ranking procedure.

e) Smaller towns have less need for, and less possibility of, major public transport operational changes. Their highway and parking needs should be assessed on a network basis against a Furness-type growth-factor exercise.

f) Larger towns usually need full transportation studies; their transportation packages are assessed on a fully integrated basis derived from a gravity modelling process.

3

Public Transport

Public Transport

By its very nature, public transport is a more efficient means of transporting large numbers of people in urban areas than is the admittedly more flexible private car. It is appropriate therefore in this consideration of comprehensive transport planning components to look first at public transport. Much that follows is related specifically to the bus but a lot of the principles are also applicable to other forms of public transport.

Public transport operations are a new field to many transport engineers and planners, and therefore warrant consideration from first principles. And the first principle to be assimilated is that, basically, people do not want to travel by public transport. They prefer the use of their own private car, which they fondly expect to take them all the way to their destination. There is therefore a fundamental problem of 'selling' public transport as a viable alternative to the private car. People must be persuaded to use public transport.

Objectives

The basic objective of any public transport undertaking is, of course, *to provide a good service to the public.* This platitude can be subdivided, and its impact thereby improved, to include the provision of:
a) a reliable and preferably quick service,
b) a convenient service,
c) a comfortable service.

Suggestions as to how these requirements can be achieved in practice will be considered later in this chapter. Briefly however, traffic management measures can frequently assist in speeding and increasing the reliability of a bus service; routeing and scheduling to minimize walking and/or waiting times together with improved bus capacities can improve the convenience and to some extent the comfort; while continuing improvements in bus design are of course essential for increased comfort in the long run.

Basic Operations

Accepting that its prime function is the movement of people in quantity, a public transport service can be divided into three operational activities:

a) collection — from widespread residential areas and/or work-places and shopping areas,

b) line haul — between residential areas and work-places and shopping areas (or from town to town),

c) distribution — to work-places and shopping areas and/or residential areas.

Any specific public transport operation, from a single route to a complete system, may include one or all of these three activities. For example, a city-centre circular bus service would consist of collection and distribution activities without line haul. Equally, a radial commuter rail route into a city would perhaps be classed as large-scale collection combined with and functioning as variable-quality line haul — no distribution being included as the train terminates at a single central station. An Inter-City train service is, of course, simply performing a line-haul activity.

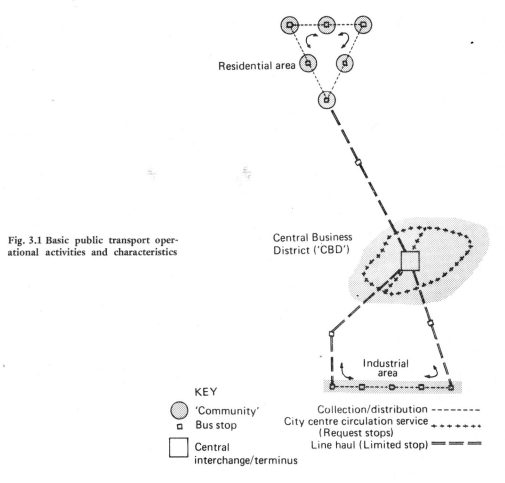

Residential area

Fig. 3.1 Basic public transport operational activities and characteristics

Central Business District ('CBD')

Industrial area

KEY

'Community'

Bus stop

Central interchange/terminus

Collection/distribution - - - - - - - -
City centre circulation service + + + + + +
(Request stops)
Line haul (Limited stop) ═══ ═══ ═══

These three operational activities are illustrated diagrammatically in Fig. 3.1, which also indicates their different characteristics:

a) Collection — frequent pick-up stops; penetration into and through housing estates rather than peripheral routeing.

b) Line haul — infrequent stops and fast-running operation. Intermediate stops on a line-haul operation reduce both its attractiveness
and its effectiveness, although of course, some stops will often be
required; the activity is seldom pure.

c) Distribution — sufficient stops rather than frequent stops; essential
need is for maximum penetration into shopping areas and work-
place areas, over-riding pedestrianization where possible and
appropriate.

Irrespective of and underlying the combination of operational
activities represented in a public transport undertaking, however, there
is also the fundamental concept of commercial operation. A public
transport undertaking provides a service to the public in return for
payment. If the service is not what the public really wants, then it will
not attract custom and therefore will not make enough money to meet
the costs of operating it.

For many years, municipal public transport undertakings have
operated on at least a break-even commercial policy, i.e. overall
revenue equalling overall expenditure. And of course, commercial bus
companies need additionally to show a profit on the capital invested.
Even where a subsidy — either hidden in the form of a government grant
towards the cost of new buses, or specific as in some rural areas — has
been paid to a bus company, this has often been treated almost as
revenue, the need to break even in commercial terms still being
applied. This commercial yardstick is perhaps the best available measure
of efficient operation, and as such, should be understood by transport
planners.

Subsidies are themselves a complicated concept, bound up with the
whole logic of public transport operating costs. Will a subsidy, for
example, actually promote a particular additional service or modal
change, or will it be used generally to bolster up a basically non-
commercial operation?

Subsidies can be thought of as means to:

a) reduce, or hold down against a rising commercial trend, the fare
levels in order to induce a public change in travel mode i.e., low,
subsidized fares to persuade people to go by bus,

b) provide an otherwise unremunerative public service, such as in rural
areas where a regular service is not commercially viable,

c) persuade the operator to provide additional services during peak
periods — again, to induce a change of mode.

The first of these approaches is that most often thought of in
comprehensive transport planning. But as will be explained later, it is
not the cost of the bus fare alone which influences a traveller's choice
of mode, but rather, the whole, generalized, cost of a journey. For a
journey involving a bus trip, the cost would include:

a) cost of time to walk to bus stop,

b) cost of time waiting at bus stop,

c) cost of time on bus,

d) cost of bus fare,

e) cost of time walking from bus stop to actual destination.

For short journeys in urban areas the cost of the bus fare can be as
little as 20 per cent of the whole journey cost. The regularity and
reliability of the service are clearly of far greater importance. Other

than as a short-term measure, a subsidy to decrease or hold down fares is not often justified.

The subsidizing of a particular service, as long as this service and its costs can be clearly identified, is often used as a means of meeting the social needs of specific geographical areas. It is usually adopted in rural areas, the alternative being no public transport service at all, and the subsidy is recognized for what it is, the meeting of a commercial short-fall for social reasons. In urban areas, this type of subsidy may be appropriate where new housing estates are being developed in phases over a period of time, and what will eventually be a viable bus service is required to be provided from the occupation of the first phase of the estate — before it is a commercial proposition.

It is with the concept of a subsidy to induce an operator to provide additional peak services that the conflict with commercial operating principles is most apparent. In commercial terms, the provision of additional peak services is often uneconomic — and therefore only to be provided if subsidized. But what, in this context, do we mean by uneconomic?

The economics of a commercially oriented public transport system are not as simple as the standard economics textbook case of supply and demand. Public transport operators experience a heavy demand for their services in the peak periods and are then left with potentially idle stock and staff for much of the rest of each day. In this condition, although extra peak services may be extremely expensive, it is possible to operate an off-peak service for little more than the bare running costs and yet be profitable — or economic.

Indeed, there are several different operating costs which need to be considered in looking at public transport operations. They are, basically:
a) fuel, repair and maintenance costs,
b) as a) plus crew wages and general administrative overheads (this cost could be of the order of 5 times cost a),
c) as b) plus servicing charges on capital and the amortization costs based on the stock *purchase* price,
d) as c) but amortization costs based on stock *replacement* prices.

Cost a) would be the marginal cost that needs to be met to make an off-peak service profitable when the alternative is for crews and stock to stand idle. If however a complete labour shift could be reduced by the cancellation of a service, then the marginal cost which needs to be met to provide that service will be cost b). During peak periods however, costs c) and d) are of course the ones which need to be met from corresponding revenue in order to ensure a break-even situation. Clearly, in healthy operating conditions, cost d) is more appropriate than cost c), which is however sometimes adopted as a criterion for non-commercial operators. Where the service is declining there may be a case for meeting only the lower cost of c), if that appears likely to meet the, at present unquantifiable, replacement requirements.

It is clear then, that the marginal cost of an additional service at the peak period is greater than in the off-peak, and Fig. 3.2 illustrates this. The reasons for this are, of course, that in the peak period the crews and the stock of either buses or trains are often fully extended; at the same time, merely because it is in the peak period, operational speeds will usually fall, increasing fuel costs, etc. Thus there is:

a) maximum stock use — an additional service may require additional stock to be purchased and additional crews to be engaged, and

b) peak operating costs — congested routes mean far less-economic operating speeds and greater wear on engines, transmissions, etc.

At the same time, any additional service in the peak period would inevitably add to any congestion already present and itself cause a further increase in operating cost. The provision, by subsidization, of an additional peak service also means the likelihood of additional idle crews, who would also need to be paid for — a wasteful use of a subsidy. The original level of peak service will have been calculated on just this sort of consideration, to develop a viable commercial operation.

Fig. 3.2 Public transport operating costs

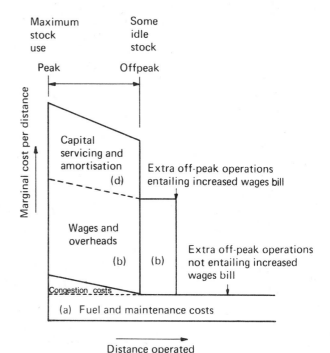

And, in any case, subsidies to provide an *extra* service in the peak period may not alone be enough to induce a change in mode by the frustrated, but comfortably cocooned, car commuter. It may well be better to initiate traffic management measures to provide bus lanes etc. which in themselves will improve the bus service. It is however thought by some that a limited shift in modal choice might be induced by an improvement in the *quality* of the peak service.

There may sometimes therefore be justification for some subsidization of a public transport system, to provide increased or improved quality stock. The provision of a capital subsidy may lead to the obviously undesirable development of a capital-intensive but less efficient system — and this must be guarded against. At other times and in other conditions, a public transport operation may already have surplus capacity of an acceptable quality, but need an operating subsidy to compensate for a very low off-peak demand. The full answer must be a flexible approach to subsidization – sometimes to provide extra services, sometimes to provide greater comfort or reliability, and occasionally to permit lower fare structures.

Irrespective of the possibility of a subsidy however, it is clearly desirable to increase the commercial viability of all the services in the peak. And a major way in which this can be done is by reducing the congestion which causes the higher basic operating cost – in part. This is a chicken-and-egg situation – if more people would travel by public transport there would be fewer cars on the roads, therefore less congestion, therefore cheaper bus operating conditions, therefore more people would travel by public transport. The problem is to break out of the cycle of cause and effect.

The passage of buses through congested urban streets can in fact be considerably improved – with a corresponding improvement in the reliability of the service – by traffic management measures. Basically, these are, in relation to buses:
a) priority over other road users (in mixed traffic flow),
b) segregation from other road users, by with- and contra-flow bus lanes, bus-only roads, etc.

Bus Priority

It has been demonstrated, in several experimental exercises, that a significant improvement in bus journey time through a signal-controlled junction can be achieved by awarding priority to buses on one phase – at Leicester for example, a right-turn-only phase. The buses are identified by selective vehicle detectors (SVD) buried beneath the road surface in a movement-segregated lane. These detectors are actuated by transponders fitted to the underside of the buses. Their identification causes the traffic signal controller, under specified conditions, to reduce the green time on the opposing phase(s) by an agreed maximum number of seconds. The opposing phase(s) are compensated for this reduction by the award of additional green time in the next cycle.

The Leicester experiment showed that although the average delay per bus was reduced by only seven seconds, the overall regularity of the service was considerably improved. There was a 24 per cent reduction in the number of buses delayed for more than a minute. In a similar project in Derby, the average peak period delay to buses through a junction was reduced by around 20 seconds per bus, and 75 per cent of all buses passed through the junction in times within a range of 9 to 31 seconds, compared with the before range of 9 to 66 seconds.

There is, of course, a small penalty to pay for this improved regularity, and it is paid by the other road users, who are delayed. This is not unacceptable, bearing in mind the objective of people-movement rather than vehicle-movement. The use of signal-controlled bus priorities at individual junctions should however be restricted to specifically appropriate locations. These are preferably where the phase attracting priority carries a low volume of traffic, with a high proportion of buses.

Bus Segregation

Of perhaps greater importance in the improvement of bus performance is the provision of bus-only lanes and busways. These can either be with the flow of the immediately adjacent traffic lane, or, in one-way streets, against the flow of the adjacent traffic flow — with-flow or contra-flow lanes — or the specific reservation of a whole road for buses only — busways.

Contra-flow bus lanes are appropriate in one-way systems to afford an easier, more direct route for buses than a possibly circuitous one-way diversionary system imposed on the rest of the traffic flow. For safety reasons it may sometimes be desirable to physically separate the contra-flow bus lane from the opposing traffic lanes by a raised median strip — taking up valuable road space. Contra-flow bus lanes, by their nature, also cause buses to track, which in turn imposes a need for a specially strengthened road surface — at additional cost. There is also a tendency for oil deposits to accumulate down the centre of a contra-flow lane, which, if nothing else, is unsightly.

One of the best-known British examples of a contra-flow bus lane is in London, on the main A10 route at Tottenham High Road, which was introduced in 1970. Because of its short length, less than 0.7 km, the regularity of the bus service did not improve significantly. The journey time for buses using the bus lane however was nearly 2½ minutes less than the 7.3 minutes for the same journey before its introduction. These times were based on a total journey length of just over a kilometre, encompassing the bus lane section.

With-flow bus lanes are often a more attractive proposition and are increasingly being implemented in British cities — particularly in London. Among the advantages of the with-flow approach are that they do not require a physical separation from the remainder of the traffic stream and, subject to the difficulty of adequate signposting, do not necessarily need to pre-empt the use of the lane for the full 24 hours of the day.

Against this of course, there remains the problem of enforcement of the with-flow traffic segregation, compared with the virtual self-policing of contra-flow lanes — but this may be largely a matter of education. To some extent however, a few violations of the segregation are not important, as long as the majority of car users respect it. Equally, it is desirable that the segregated lanes are sufficiently utilized to earn their keep. It is sometimes useful therefore to consider the use of the bus lane by taxis as well as by buses. There is also the suggestion that bus lanes, if provided with lay-bys for stops, might also be used by non-stopping heavy commercial vehicles.

While considering the question of adequate utilization of bus lanes it is appropriate also to remember once again that transport planning is correctly an overall, comprehensive process. Buses should not therefore be favoured at *excessive* expense to other road users — at least without careful consideration of the likely effects, and acknowledgement of them. This is particularly important at signal-controlled junctions incorporating with-flow bus lanes on one or more approaches. The Transport and Road Research Laboratory have shown, in their Report LR 448, that if a bus lane included in a three-lane approach is carried right up to the STOP line then the buses save about half a minute in travel time compared with a no-bus-lane junction. At the same time however, this total-bus-lane approach reduces the overall capacity of the junction by around 30 per cent.

By terminating the bus lane a certain distance back from the STOP line it was possible, however, to save very nearly the same bus travel time and yet allow the junction capacity to revert to virtually (approximately 95 per cent) that of the without-bus-lane condition. The distance back from the STOP line at which the bus lane should be terminated for the optimum condition was apparently dependent on the green time of the bus approach aspect of the signal, at tentatively 2 metres per second of green time.

With-flow bus lanes of varying lengths have been in operation in several countries for some years. A considerable number have been in use in Paris since the mid 1960s, affording increases of 4 to 10 km/h in bus speeds, at the expense of other road users. Britain's first with-flow lane was London's Vauxhall Bridge central lane scheme, operating in the evening peak period only, with flows of 85 buses per hour. This scheme showed considerable savings in bus travel times together with an increased overall capacity and traffic speed. These figures however are distorted by the removal of central bollards to provide effectively an *extra* bus lane.

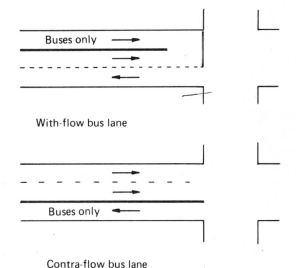

With-flow bus lane

Fig. 3.3 Contra- and with-flow bus lanes

Contra-flow bus lane

Extending the concept of bus segregation still further, the obvious conclusion must be bus-only roads — busways. Within an *existing* system of urban roads there are clearly a limited number of locations where this approach is worthwhile. A major problem in introducing an urban busway within the existing urban network will be the restriction of access thereby imposed on frontagers; short lengths of busways are therefore the usual rule. The logic of introducing a busway into existing systems is usually either because the road is too narrow to permit a bus lane in conjunction with other traffic, or when bus penetration into a pedestrian precinct is desirable.

Busways are of greater importance in new urban developments where the whole transportation system can be planned from the start, or where, for example, abandoned urban railway rights-of-way can be used to superimpose an up-to-date transport system on the urban fabric. In these conditions a whole network of busways can be introduced, with maximum penetration into both residential and shopping or industrial areas. Runcorn New Town is an example of a busway system incorporated in a new development.

The Runcorn Busway System

Runcorn New Town has been designed around the concept of a busway system.

All new houses are within 450 metres, or 5 minutes walk, of a busway stop.

Ultimately, 20 km of specially built busway, in figure-of-eight form, through central 'Shopping City'.

Busways normally 6.7 m wide but 6.1 m on viaduct sections — all fully segregated, fenced, etc.

Single-decker, one-man-operated (OMO) buses, scheduled at 30-35 km/h.

All bus stops have shelters with timetables and fare structure displayed.

Graduated fare structure with fare-box collection — no tickets.

Fixed-interval scheduling — in 1973, 4 routes on an incomplete network, offer 5, 4, 1, and 1 services per hour respectively, so combined that remote terminals have 2 buses per hour and the central area, 10 per hour.

1973 services operated by 5 buses.

In central area, busways elevated. Outside central area, at grade. Busways cross estate roads at grade with signal-controlled junctions, with absolute bus priority if approached at correct speed.

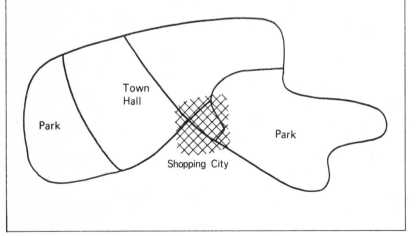

Linked, or Individual, Bus Segregation Schemes?

In existing towns and cities it is possible, and undoubtedly attractive, to envisage linking individual lengths of bus lanes and busways to provide a continuous network of bus-segregated routes. This approach, however, is not necessarily appropriate when considered in a comprehensive transport context. Not all sections of a bus route are so congested that they will afford significant benefit to the bus by segregation. Yet this segregation, if imposed, could well itself cause congestion for the rest of the road users using the thereby restricted road width. While the overall approach is worthy of consideration − it may be acceptable deliberately to delay other road users even though the benefit to public transport is negligible − the alternative of unlinked bus lanes at congested locations only should also be investigated.

In London, a series of general criteria has been developed for the selection of possible bus priority or segregation schemes, which are clearly appropriate for other such scheme selection. To justify further detailed study, a scheme was expected to:

a) give a significant advantage to bus operations,
b) have a negligible effect on total traffic capacity, and not cause secondary congestion,
c) yield a net benefit to the community,
d) cost as little as possible,
e) be enforceable,
f) minimize adverse effects on pedestrians, frontagers, and the adjacent environment,
g) be capable of early implementation,
h) assist flow of other traffic as far as possible,
i) have an economic life.

Staffing Considerations

Delays and irregularities in bus operations due to congestion and the general presence of other road users are not the sole major cause of reduced bus journey speeds in large towns and cities. Major delays are also attributable to the essential stops for loading and unloading of passengers. A survey carried out in London over a central-area section of a route used by buses with 2-man crews, shows that around ten per cent of the total journey time was taken up by loading and unloading. A similar survey on a one-man-operated (OMO), fixed fare service, although operated at faster running speeds, showed virtually no change in comparable journey time, due to an increase in loading and unloading time to about twenty per cent. These facts emphasize the importance of the staffing problems experienced by many public transport operators. Shortage of staff and the high labour cost element in operating costs are accelerating moves towards one-man operation of services, which will be cheaper to operate but often slower, due to the longer loading and unloading times (which will partly depend on the fare structure and collection system, see below). It is therefore more appropriate, where staffing conditions permit, to use OMO services in outer areas rather than in congested city centres.

Despite the use of OMO buses wherever appropriate, many major cities are experiencing a serious shortage of bus crews as well as the equally widespread shortage of maintenance staff. The overall general problems of relative wage levels in public service undertakings compared to some sectors of private industry are well-known − and discussion on these is outside the scope of this book. An interesting side effect of the

---

Comparison of One-Man and Two-Man Operated Buses
(Summarized from TRRL Report LR 521)

Average stop times on urban routes show one-man-operated (OMO) buses stop more than 100 per cent longer than 2-man operated buses (20 sec: 8 sec)

From any type of bus, the alighting time per passenger is about 1½ seconds.

Boarding time:
  a) for two-man operated buses is not usually more than 2 seconds per passenger,
  b) for OMO buses can be as high as 6 seconds per passenger, dependent on fare collection system.

Use of fare boxes and no-change policies reduces OMO boarding time considerably. Fare boxes could save up to 2½ seconds and a no-change policy about ½ second per passenger (7½ seconds and 1½ seconds per average stop).

Use of season tickets or passes saves about 1½ seconds boarding time per passenger (4½ seconds per average stop).

Use of a mechanically operated centre exit door increases unusable or dead time by as much as 6 seconds per stop.

---

introduction of bus-only lanes is that the more effective bus operation improves crew morale and in turn, marginally improves staffing conditions.

Fare Structures and Collection Systems

A major part of the avoidable delays at loading and unloading stops and/or the necessity for 2-man crews, is due to the fare-collection systems. Traditionally and obviously, public transport fares have in the past been based, in a series of coin-dictated steps, on the necessary revenue per unit route distance. Inevitably, this has meant the fare-collector needing to know the inter-stage fares and to provide change for proffered coins — the passenger not needing to know the fare, merely to pay as demanded. It was the responsibility of the fare-collector to ensure that all fares were collected.

With driver fare collection and the effect this has on bus boarding times, the traditional fare structure/collection systems needed rethinking. Alternative fare structures, other than the obvious and necessary simplification and reduction of the existing steps, basically consist of:

flat-fare system,
free service.

A major problem in introducing an overall flat-fare system is that of fixing the actual fare level. To fix it, on economic/commercial grounds, at the average of present fare collections, will penalize the very large number of, often poorer, short-distance travellers and effectively subsidize the possibly more affluent longer-distance travellers. To fix

The Stevenage 'Superbus'

Features

45-seat single-decker buses, with 15 standee spaces.

4.7 km route length.

One-man operation.

Flat fare systems, with multi-tickets purchasable off vehicle (same price).

Well publicized, clear time-tables.

Fixed-interval scheduling — 5 minutes peak and off-peak, 10 minutes evenings and weekends.

Distinctive yellow and blue livery and catch-name 'SUPERBUS'

Direct routing, no detours.

Laybys and shelters at all stops — all stops 'Request'.

Bus stops sited for maximum 5-minute walk from dwellings.

Results (up to July 1972)

Large increase in peak period patronage — 37% increase in 15 months.

Larger increase in total journeys by bus — more than 100% increase in 15 months.

Significant reduction in car work-journeys — 2.7% of drivers and 2.7% of car passengers.

Reduced passenger waiting time at stops.

Immediate popularity of multi-ticket issues — 8% of total fares within three weeks.

Boarding time, previously 1—1½ seconds per passenger with 2-man crews, rose to 9 seconds per passenger initially, but has now stabilized at 2½—5 seconds per passenger, depending on location and time of day.

A viable, subsidized service

it at other than a commercially viable average level means a need for a probably large and almost certainly continuing subsidy.

The introduction of a free public transport service obviously does away with all fare collection problems. The saving from that however is likely to be only of the order of ten per cent of the total service operating costs — with residual costs having to be met by either the rate-payers or the tax-payers. Nothing is really free — someone has to pay. In late 1972 the Greater London Council estimated that a free public transport service in London would cost about £130 million and add 20p in the pound to the rates. A further disadvantage of the free service approach is the inevitable attraction of additional short trippers who would otherwise have walked — thereby increasing the load on the system unnecessarily.

A major side effect of the adoption of a free fare system has been recognized in studies of London, where British Rail services duplicate some London Transport routes. If London Transport were to introduce a free fare system there would probably be a very sizeable switch of passengers away from British Rail. Even if British Rail were to reduce the fares on its duplicated routes by a massive 75 per cent, it has been calculated that there would still be something of the order of a 25 per cent switch to London Transport.

Because of the problems and disadvantages of both flat and free fare systems — on other than parts of a transport service, such as a flat fare central area service — it is likely that a simplified stepped fare structure will often be appropriate, and adopted, for many transport services. With the stepped fare structure, a major assistance to any collection system can be afforded by the simple display at each bus stop of the fares from that stop to all major destinations, preferably together with a stylized map of each service route using the stop.

With both flat and stepped fare structures the collection still remains a problem. Measures appropriate to the alleviation of the problem include:

a) Self-service fare collection/ticket issuing machinery or fare-controlled entry gate.

b) No-change payment to driver — who may issue ticket, or release entry gate.

c) Associated with b) — use of a fare box; the passenger drops in the fare, in any combination of coins, and the driver can see at a glance its correctness.

d) Pre-purchased tickets — used either as entry-gate passes or, better, checked at random, but frequently, as on the Continent — where boarding and disembarking times are thereby considerably reduced.

e) Season tickets (fare contracts).

f) Go-as-you-please (Rover) tickets — for specified periods and/or for part or whole systems. On their own, these tickets are of little impact in saving time unless of almost universal use.

A common problem with virtually all measures for improved fare collection is that of the elderly traveller, the child (possibly with reduced fares) and the stranger to the area. All of these classes of traveller are at a disadvantage in possibly not understanding or even being able to operate the self-service system, not knowing or having the correct fare, nor having pre-purchased a ticket. A single passenger can considerably increase the loading delay at a stop and throw the whole service off schedule.

Bus Sizes

Another factor influencing the efficiency of a bus service is the size of the bus itself. It has been suggested that once the crew wages have to be met, the ideal would be to have a big bus and fill it as full as possible. This approach, however, ignores the total operating costs, the effect of larger vehicles on the rest of the traffic flow (i.e. an increase in the effective pcu value compared with the standard bus pcu value), and the increased delays to all traffic caused by the longer loading and un-loading stops of the larger bus in unsegregated conditions. As a result of detailed study under a wide variety of simulated conditions of private traffic restraint, it has been suggested that the optimum bus is likely to be a 40- to 50-seater, double-decker carrying 24 to 30 passengers (60 per cent occupancy) on average.

It is most important for the reputation of a bus service that the vehicles provide adequate capacity for waiting passengers. To plan on 60 per cent occupancy is therefore a realistic approach, allowing overload potential. Further overload potential, provided by vehicle design for standees, is also desirable.

Interchanges

Before moving on to a brief review of possible future public transport developments, it is appropriate once again to recall that the real problem is transportation as a whole, and not just the consideration of public transport. And this means that an integrated approach must be developed — there are other forms of transport than buses.

In the context of bus public transport the integration relates largely to:
a) mode interchanges, where bus services providing collection and/or distribution facilities link with rail or bus line-haul services, or
b) park-and-ride interchanges, where car parks are provided on the edges of a central urban area with free or subsidized bus services into the central area.
(Park-and-ride facilities will be further considered in the chapter on Parking.)

The basic essentials of a public transport interchange are:
a) The interchange should be covered, i.e. roofed, and preferably fully enclosed.
b) The interchange should provide adequate platform/bay space for the services using it.
c) The walking distances entailed in changing route or mode should be kept to a minimum, possibly by the use of multi-level facilities.
d) The interchange should be located conveniently for the town or city centre, where appropriate.
e) The facilities and platform/bay locations should be clearly and adequately signposted.
f) Adequate comfortable waiting space should be provided, preferably with refreshment facilities.

The possibilities of linking such an interchange building with a car park and/or shopping facilities should not be overlooked — the parking aspect will also be further considered in the chapter on Parking.

A simpler interchange facility might perhaps be considered for the transfer of passengers from suburban collector services to an express line-haul service from the suburb to the central area. This sort of linked service, however, is often not a viable proposition – depending on the length of the line-haul section – because passengers understandably object to a transfer from bus to bus on the grounds of wasted time and additional delay. This is aggravated by the increased cost value that passengers assign to waiting time compared with actual travel time. This aggravation cost in turn increases the overall journey cost, thereby reducing the possibility of the desired change in mode from private to public transport. As far as bus-to-bus transfers are concerned therefore, only rural buses need normally be catered for by other than a simple bus stop.

The simplest, and in some ways the most important, interchange facility is the individual bus stop, where the pedestrian waits to become transformed into a passenger. A draughty street corner with a sign indicating 'Bus Stop' is not adequate, nor sufficient to induce comfortable motorists to change their mode to bus travel. Simple shelters should, and usually could, be provided at *all* bus stops – at least partially enclosed, vandal-proof and, on remoter routes, provided with simple bench seats. As already mentioned, easily understood details of route and fares should be displayed, but ample space will remain for possible advertising use, making the shelter virtually free.

Rural Bus Services

Rural bus services have different problems from those in urban areas. There is no massive peak period demand with a falling-off in the off-peak. In fact, there is seldom any massive demand at all. The affluent society has meant a switch to car travel for many rural travellers, just as for their cousins in town; and there is no great transport planning need to induce them to switch back.

The rural bus service is provided almost exclusively for the less fortunate people who do not have access to a car. And there will be such people for many years to come – the no-car-owners and the one-car-owners whose one car is in use by the head of the household, leaving his wife with no transport other than the bus. It should be remembered that the highest long-term forecast – saturation level – of car ownership is only 0.45 cars per head of population. In the 1970-80 decade, the car ownership is expected to rise, on average, to at most 0.36 cars per head.

On a public utility or social commitment basis, a bus service should obviously be provided in rural areas. But the demand is often insufficient to permit the operation of a commercially viable service. Is it then right to subsidize a full traditional service for what is perhaps only a small number of people? Clearly, depending on numbers and costs, it is sometimes appropriate to subsidize such a service. In other instances it is not, and other approaches have to be adopted, such as combining rural public transport with other public services, e.g. mail deliveries (the 'post-bus') 'meals-on-wheels', etc. In some rural areas a properly organized car-sharing pool or system of 'available lifts' may be an answer worth considering.

Certainly, in most rural areas where traditional services are only marginally viable, it is worth investigating the use of, among other ideas, mini-buses, one-man operation, and the concept of village buses. This latter concept involves basing a mini-bus and driver on a village and arranging a wide variety of services for the bus to provide, from regular connecting services to the line-haul bus service, to special shopping or market excursions once a week.

Perhaps most important of all, in rural areas as in the towns, is a regular and reliable timetable. If people know that every x hours at y minutes past the hour there will be a bus, they will react favourably. Uncertainty will cause frustration and even, in the long term, an increase in the urban drift.

Dial-a-Ride

The real transportation problem, however, is more in the urban areas than in the rural ones. And on the fringe of this field, i.e. towns rather than cities, perhaps the most original new development, breaking away from the traditional concept of publicized, or at least implied, scheduled service operations, is what is known variously as Dial-a-bus, Dial-a-Ride, or, in America, D-A-R-T (Demand Activated Rapid Transit). Much of the development work on the use and application of the Dial-a-Ride system, both in America and in Britain, has been done by the Ford Motor Company.

The full Dial-a-Ride system depends fundamentally on the completely flexible routing and scheduling of small buses in response to telephone requests, most effectively in the off-peak period. By serving a number of passengers all moving in the same general direction, the cost of the service can be kept at a fairly low level — higher than a normally scheduled and routed bus, but considerably lower than a comparable taxi fare.

A potential Dial-a-Ride passenger telephones in a request to be picked up, stating also his destination and the number of passengers. At the control centre, the details of the required service are fed into a computer (the use of which is essential to all but the very simplest and cheapest of Dial-a-Ride operations) which maintains details of all unfilled requests, of the last-known location of all buses in the system and of the required destinations of their passengers. Taking all of this information into account, the computer is programmed to select the most suitable bus to fill the request, and to suitably amend its route.

The buses are all equipped with two-way radios and a digital print-out device, and at every loading/unloading stop the next destination is advised by the computer. Within its specified area of operation, which may be a sector of a town or the whole town, the service offers a standard and guaranteed maximum waiting time and maximum journey time — these factors being inputs to the computer as constraints on its routing choice.

Within the concept of a demand-responsive bus service as explained above, there are different levels of service which can be offered. The highest level, as already described, can be designated as many-to-many, meaning that the service operates from a virtually unrestricted series of pick-up points to a similar range of destinations, over an unrestricted network of roads within a specified area. A lesser level, but one which nevertheless offers a very useful service, is the many-to-few approach, where passengers are picked up over a whole area for carriage to one or more fixed destinations such as railway stations etc.

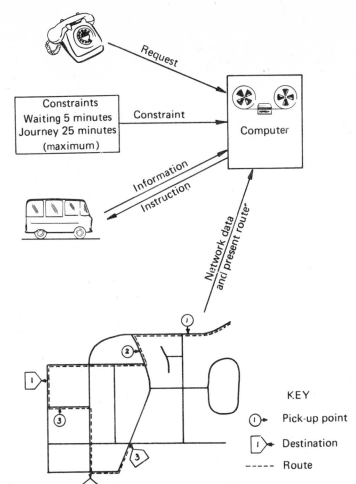

Fig. 3.4 The concept of 'Dial-a-Ride'

Another viable and simpler alternative is for the buses to operate on a predetermined route, diverting on demand and at extra charge, to collect passengers from houses within a specified width corridor, the bus returning to the route at the point where it left it. The overall route time is adequate to permit the diversion time being made up before the destination is reached.

Many-to-few systems are already in operation in several locations, such as Maidstone, while the route-corridor-collection system has been very successful in America, at Mansfield, Ohio, and is planned for Harlow in Essex. Several British many-to-many services are being planned but have not, at the time of writing, been implemented.

Public Transport other than Buses

Other than buses, there are only a few public transport systems likely to be viable in the foreseeable future. There are the various types of Light Rail Rapid Transit (LRRT) systems — the London Underground and the Paris Metro being well-known examples. Newer systems for use in smaller urban areas than the really major conurbations could well be light-weight, electrically-powered, single- or multi-car OMO trains, running on twin-rail track such as is used for the Continental U-bahn networks and the proposed rapid transit system for Britain's Tyneside.

The major disadvantage of LRRT compared with a bus/busway system is its lack of flexibility. An LRRT system cannot readily be extended into new development areas, and in fact, must to some extent depend on bus feeder services for its own profitable operation.

The other possible major innovation in public transport within the medium-term future is that exemplified by the British Minitram system. Similar overseas systems include the American Airtrans system at Dallas Fort Worth airport and the Morgantown PRT project, and the French Tridim and VAL systems. Evolved by the TRRL from the earlier CabTrack proposal, Minitram, like the other systems, is a fixed, segregated-track, driverless, computer-controlled vehicle system, designed to operate at, above, or below grade, with frequent stops. Minitram envisages a 10-15 seat vehicle, operating singly or in multi-car trains, at as little as 15-second headways. Both the light channel-type track and the Minitram vehicle itself are designed to be as small and unobtrusive as possible, reducing its urban environmental impact to a minimum. An experimental Minitram installation is expected to be in operation in Sheffield by the early 1980s.

Comparison of Alternative Future Public Transport Systems

Considerations	Bus/Busways	LRRT	Minitram etc.
Flexibility	Buses can leave busways and penetrate devt. areas	Needs bus feeder services. Cannot be readily extended	As for LRRT but slightly more flexible
Staffing	OMO = minimum	Basically OMO, but possibility of fully auto.	Fully automatic
Passenger capacity per vehicle	Up to 60 per bus	80 sitting 80 standing per double-unit	15 per vehicle
Practical headways	40 seconds (segregated)	90 seconds	15 seconds
Hourly capacity of one-way track at minimum headway	7 000 pass/hr	10-15 000 pass/hr	10 000 pass/hr
Maximum speeds	30-35 km/h incl. stopping time	80 km/h	50-60 km/h

For shorter-distance urban movements, the concept of a moving pavement is often considered. Moving pavements have been in (very limited) use all over the world for many years — as early as 1893 in Chicago. The problems preventing their wider use have always been concerned with the speed of movement and the associated difficulties in boarding and alighting. These are now hopefully being alleviated by the Batelle 'Integrator', which is a device whereby boarding passengers are gradually speeded up from a safe boarding speed to an economic travel speed before transfer to the actual travelator. This boarding system does, however, reduce the flexibility of this system by restricting boarding to 'Integrator' locations.

There can be little doubt, however, that for some years to come, and in most towns and rural areas, the bus, supported by certain commuter- and rural-train services, will be the main form of public transport, for other than major inter-city movements. Underground railways and other forms of LRRT will have their role in the larger cities and in these large urban areas there may well be a role for the newer developments too — but even then, very definitely, *alongside* the bus.

SUMMARY

a) The public need *persuading* to use public transport rather than the private car. A major form of persuasion is to offer a reliable, regular, convenient and comfortable service, at an acceptable price.

b) Subsidies may sometimes be justified, especially as a temporary measure, in order to ensure better public transport services, but they should never vitiate the commercial approach to public transport operations.

c) All public transport systems consist of a combination or selection of: collection, line haul, and distribution operations.

d) Bus operations can be improved by contra- and with-flow bus-only lanes, by bus priorities at junctions, etc., and by busways.

e) The one-man operation of buses gives significant savings in labour costs but unless fare structure and fare collection systems are carefully selected, may cause longer journey times — due to increased loading times.

f) The proper design of public transport interchanges, including those for park-and-ride operations, is an essential part of efficient public transport operations, because of the added 'weight' that passengers attribute to useless waiting time.

g) Dial-a-Ride appears to offer a flexible, useful advance over the traditionalism of fully scheduled services and may be worth considering in appropriate locations.

h) Despite new developments such as Minitram and the travelator, bus public transport is likely to be of most importance for some years to come.

4

Traffic Management

Throughout this book, the inter-relationship of the several aspects of transportation planning on a county-wide basis is apparent — and emphasized. This integration is further demonstrated in the field of traffic management, with its involvement in bus priority measures, parking restraints, pedestrianization, etc.

Objectives

Before continuing however, let us first clarify what is meant by traffic management. Fundamentally, the objective of traffic management is to ensure the *overall* best use of the existing urban transport facilities, subject to the constraints of environmental preservation and public acceptability. This 'best use' — which may or may not be the *maximum* use, or that generating the *maximum benefits* — involves the imposition upon the traveller of rules and regulations governing the use of transport facilities. It may also involve new works and improvements of limited scale, capable of early implementation. Traffic management measures are usually relatively inexpensive, and frequently achieve impressive short-term economic benefits. (We have specified *urban* facilities above because this is generally the field in which traffic management is of greatest significance, but we shall see how several of the basic principles can also be employed in rural conditions.)

Perhaps the most important aspect of traffic management is its major involvement in the efficient use of basically existing facilities. Should significant expenditure be involved in new facilities then this is almost certainly outside the scope of what is generally understood to be traffic management. However, the definition of 'significant expenditure' is a difficult one when, for example, area traffic control schemes can cost up to a million pounds — yet are clearly 'traffic management'.

Let us say then that traffic management measures should:
a) be relatively inexpensive and capable of early implementation,
b) improve the performance/capacity of existing transport facilities,
c) reduce the incidence of accidents — or at least, prevent an increase,
d) improve — or at least protect — the state of the urban environment,
e) be sufficiently flexible to adapt to minor land-use changes, to the later construction of new roads, to the adoption of new public transport measures, and to the development of new parking policies,
f) where appropriate, generate adequate economic benefits to warrant their implementation.

41

Surveys

Before any move is made to initiate traffic-management measures it is
essential that adequate information is available on present-day travel
patterns. Without this information it is not possible to make a
sensible choice from the available techniques. The sort of information
that is required is origin/destination matrices of travel within the area
under consideration, average network journey times by individual
sections or links, parking availability and demand, public transport
usage and service reliability, and general accident data.

It is clear that this information is virtually identical with that which
would be required for either a full transportation study or for a
simpler, small-town growth-factor exercise. This clearly argues for the
integration of traffic management investigations into the overall
context of transportation studies of all kinds. Equally it is appropriate
at this stage also to clarify the function of traffic management measures
within the overall framework of transportation planning. Because large,
capital-intensive transportation proposals inevitably entail several years
of preparatory work and planning, and because of the time involved in
the planning process itself, there is often a hiatus in transport planning
implementation at the start of a plan period. This gap can well be
filled by an Immediate Action Programme determined from study of
the initial planning surveys and comprising relatively inexpensive
traffic management measures. This is not to imply, however, that
traffic management measures are *solely* appropriate to these early
years — merely that a significant proportion of the measures will have a
greater impact early rather than late.

Accepting then that traffic management measures will fill the
implementation gap in the early years of a transport plan, it is appropriate to investigate on the basis of an early implementation date.
Whereas most county-wide transportation planning is geared to a
design date at the end of a 15-year plan period, it is obviously more
sensible to base Immediate Action traffic management measures on a
5-year design period. Over this period of time there is little justification
for varying, zone to zone, the growth of travel demands. A study-wide
factoral basis for growth is quite adequate — subject of course to any
specific local amendment to allow for a major zonal change, such as the
opening of a major shopping complex on the site of a 'non-traffic-
generator'.

Survey requirements specific to the design of traffic management
measures which may not be included in the overall survey procedures
will be concerned largely with the central shopping area. Pedestrian
walk-trips and other central, intra-zonal movements, neither of which
are adequately picked up in the main surveys, should be surveyed as a
separate exercise. It is also possible that the main surveys will intend
little more than a cursory investigation of accident patterns — these too
should be surveyed as a separate, traffic-management oriented, exercise.
'Path- and kerb-side' and parking lot surveys will frequently be adequate
for the first of these exercises while the average local authority
engineer's office will probably have an ongoing accident-recording
system in operation. This, backed up by police records, will usually be
all that is required for the traffic management accident survey.

Future Prediction Factors

The base year surveys complete, travel demands as indicated in OD matrices by mode can be factored to the short-term design year, 5 years ahead — say 1981 for the purpose of this exercise. Private vehicle mode travel patterns can be projected forward by the use of Tanner Factors (Chap. 2) — or simpler, 5 per cent per annum growth — but this is not an appropriate method for the future factoring of travel patterns by public transport.

Over a recent 10-year period the decline in the total number of passenger journeys by stage services — as opposed to express services, excursions or contract hirings — has been an average of around 3 to 4 per cent per annum (Source: Passenger Transport in Great Britain 1971). The lower figure relates more to large urban areas while the higher figure relates to all stage services. It would therefore seem appropriate, in the absence of comparably valid local data, to project the base year public transport demand matrix forward by applying a decline rate of 3 per cent per annum. (Though this decline rate may be acceptable for this relatively short projection of trends, it is not necessarily appropriate for longer-range forecasting, and should not be used in that context without further consideration.)

Once the short-term future travel patterns have been established, and the general patterns modified to allow significant local changes, the future trouble spots and bottlenecks can be identified. From this exercise it will be possible to prepare comprehensive short-term traffic management proposals for consideration and assessment.

The techniques that are at present available from which to develop the comprehensive traffic management proposals are, in random order:

a) road-paint measures — lane lines, direction markings, road signs etc.,
b) one-way systems, including minor gyratories,
c) pedestrian safety measures — crossings, guard-rails etc.,
d) on-street parking controls — including institution of clearways,
e) improved junction controls — both signals and roundabouts,
f) linking of traffic signals — area traffic control,
g) pedestrianization measures — perhaps with bus penetration,
h) bus priority measures — bus lanes, busways, bus priorities,
i) lorry routes etc.

(Bus revenue support is also appropriate but is dealt with in Chapter 3.)

Road-Paint Measures

Road-paint measures, fundamental to all traditional traffic engineering, are generally well-known and already adopted in many urban areas throughout the country. Surprisingly however, there are still areas where the application of a few lines on the road would significantly ease the movement of traffic. The basic function of road-paint traffic management measures is to *inform* the driver — to guide him into the correct lane for the movement he wants to make; to ensure that he is not left to wonder which route is the one he wants; to persuade him to use the full width of available road space.

And, although most towns are at least aware of the uses and advantages of lines on the road, very many are still inadequate in respect of internal road signs. How often has every driver become lost in passing through a strange town — when the road signs he is following peter out, or are, to him anyway, ambiguous! This sort of thing is of greatest impact in the larger towns and conurbations but can be equally frustrating in smaller towns and in the county at large. More use should be made of repeater route signs and identification of the major road at minor junctions. Important traffic attractors should be identified and signposted. The regulations exist, all that is required is the initiative to use them. It is important to remember that a confused or lost driver will travel slowly and indecisively — increasing congestion and delaying whole traffic streams. It is better by far to help him before he causes the delay.

Within the concept, if not the practice, of road-paint measures, should also be included the banning of right turns. These can be replaced by 'Q' (preferably) or 'P' turns, resulting in impressive delay and accident savings. Through-road capacity is likely to be increased by at least 15 per cent. A similar measure, more appropriate to road-paint practice, is the use of box junctions, where a yellow-paint-hatched box is marked in the junction with the intention of preventing the junction from locking across. This measure too is highly effective — in appropriate locations.

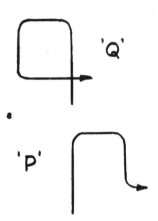

One-way Systems

Following along the same line of traditional traffic engineering management measures, the implementation of one-way systems will, as is well known, increase the capacity of existing roads by around 50 per cent. It will also reduce the likelihood of accidents, by reducing the number of points of conflict at intersections. It will also lead to an increase in speed, although possibly also to a system-wide decrease in overall journey speed due to the longer distances involved.

The one major factor which is often inadequately considered in the implementation of one-way systems is, however, the environmental impact on the lesser roads brought into the system by the introduction of the gyratory. Residential streets become through roads, residential parking becomes impossible, the quality of life deteriorates. This does not always happen — it is sufficient for the transport planner to be alert to the possibility and guard against it.

Pedestrian Safety Measures

Taking a thoroughly jaundiced and narrow viewpoint, accidents cause congestion and traffic hold-ups. If for no other reason — and human-itarian reasons are of course far more important — it therefore behoves the transport planner to reduce accidents, and particularly so in urban areas, where the hold-ups are likely to be most severe. And the way to prevent most personal injury accidents at any rate is to segregate pedestrians from vehicles. So, once again, we are back to traditional traffic engineering.

Pedestrian/vehicle segregation can be in space or in time, or by physical barriers — which are effectively merely an enforcement of spatial segregation. Segregation in space means expensive subways and pedestrian bridges — neither of which are popular with pedestrians unless the distance from A to B via subway or bridge is shorter, or more convenient, than the direct, at-grade distance. And this proviso implies major construction works based on area-wide design concepts, which will usually put these measures out of our already defined limits of traffic management in this context. Of course, segregation in space by subways and bridges can be enforced by physical barriers, such as guard-rails. This in turn however may lead to the more agile pedestrians climbing over the rail, causing perhaps a greater accident risk than if no rail had been present!

More appropriate measures, in the present context, to permit pedestrians to cross roads without conflict with the traffic are of course the Zebra, and the more recent Pelican crossings. Both of these are forms of segregation in time, inasmuch as a vehicle is not legally permitted to use the road crossing space at the same time as the pedestrian is using it. Provided that the traffic and pedestrian flows are sufficient to justify its installation, the Pelican is a better form of crossing than the Zebra. This is because of the added safety of a positive time period for all classes of road user, and because the Pelican restricts the delay to vehicles to a reasonable limit. It is relevant to note that Pelican crossings generally reduce accidents by around 60 per cent compared

Pedestrian Crossings

The Department of the Environment's (at that time, the Min. of Tpt.) Circular Roads 20/68 and the subsequent Addendum dated 20 Sept. 1968 specifies the conditions appropriate for the installation of Pelican crossings.

Pelican crossings are likely to be appropriate when:

a) light pedestrian flows experience difficulty in crossing a heavy vehicle flow,
b) vehicle flows experience difficulty in moving due to very heavy pedestrian flows — e.g. outside sports grounds, railway stations, etc.,
c) vehicle speeds are so high that pedestrian confidence in a Zebra crossing is insufficient.

The pedestrian/vehicle conflict criteria which should at least be reached to justify a Pelican crossing are:

V(veh/h)*		1400	1200	1000	800	600
P(ped/h)*	no refuge	50	250	500	750	1000
	with refuge	100	400	700	1000	

* All flows are totals in both directions based on an average of 4 peak hours in a 24-hour period, the pedestrian counts being made over a 100-metre length of road centred on the proposed crossing site.

The basic criterion for justification of Zebra crossings is that pedestrian and vehicle flows, measured in similar conditions to those specified above, when applied to the relation PV^2 should at least equal 10^8, or 2×10^8 if a central refuge is available. This criterion would be varied however in certain conditions — accepting lower values in a small town or village and requiring higher values in city centres.

with a previous Zebra crossing at the same location. In busy central areas Zebra crossings can cause excessive delays to vehicles because of their non-limitation of pedestrian use. The installation cost of a Pelican, at around £1000 for a 25-year life, at 1970 prices, is approximately double that of a Zebra. Annual costs, covering capital, maintenance and running costs over the expected life of a crossing are of the order of £100 per annum for Pelicans and £70 per annum for Zebras.

The use of guard-rails in conjunction with Zebra or Pelican crossings can be of marked effect in reducing accidents — which are liable to be about three times greater within about 50 metres of the crossing than actually on it. (Probably about three times higher risk.) The guard-rails when installed, should extend for a minimum of 10 metres on either side of the crossings. The recent zig-zag road markings prohibiting overtaking and parking on approaches to crossings will also reduce accidents.

Parking Controls

A further traffic management measure, well-known to practising traffic engineers, is the control or prohibition of on-street parking. This is more comprehensively dealt with in the chapter on parking, but the concept of peak-hour parking control — urban clearways — is more appropriate to traffic management and should be mentioned here.

Parked vehicles inevitably reduce the available road width and hence the capacity of any road. What is less well known, other than by specialist traffic engineers, however, is the magnitude of the effect of just a few parked vehicles. Just three vehicles parked along a one kilometre stretch of road effectively reduces the carriageway width by 0.9 metres, with a 200 pcu/h, or 16 per cent, loss of capacity. Figure 4.1 illustrates the impact of parked vehicles in terms of effective road width.

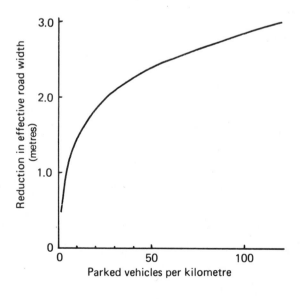

Fig. 4.1 The relationship of numbers of parked vehicles to effective road width

As most congestion and delays occur in the morning and evening peak periods, it is often sufficient, at least in the short-term, which is the prescribed province of traffic management, to ban all stationary vehicles on traffic-significant radial and other routes during these periods. And the use of the phrase 'all stationary vehicles' rather than 'parking' was specific, to cover loading, unloading and just plain stopping to pick someone up. The adoption of peak-hour urban clearways does imply that buses too should preferably not stop on the road — which means the provision of laybys where appropriate.

The object of parking controls and restrictions in the traffic management context, however, is to allow or enhance the free flow of traffic. This is a different objective from the use of parking controls as a form of traffic restraint — which is the approach dealt with in Chapter 5. Both approaches have their integrated roles in comprehensive transport planning.

Improved Junction Controls

However, improvements to the use of the road space by means of peak-hour clearways and the like do not tackle the problem of congestion at junctions — which is of greater importance than the delays between junctions. And perhaps the most significant recent advance in junction control has been the so-called mini roundabout which effectively provides a greater capacity for flow through a junction than traditional designs, yet within the constraints of the existing outer highway boundaries. Mini rounadbouts can of course be designed for and implemented in new installations — as they are increasingly used — but it is their ability to increase the throughput of an existing junction which is appropriate to this consideration of traffic management measures. Capacity increases of 25 per cent are commonly obtained by conversion to mini roundabouts and at some sites considerably greater improvements have been observed.

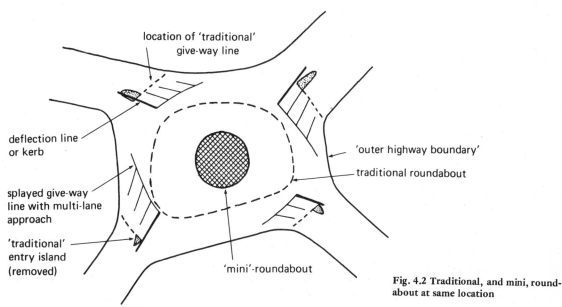

Fig. 4.2 Traditional, and mini, roundabout at same location

Capacity of Mini Roundabouts

The Department of the Environment's Technical Memorandum H7/71 of 3 June 1971 gives the capacity of the new layout roundabouts as:

$$Q = K(\Sigma W + \sqrt{A})$$

where Q = total entry volume in pcu/h.

ΣW = the sum of the basic road widths of the approaches to the junction used by traffic in both directions, i.e. the full road width, not the half-width approach, measured in metres.

A = the gross intersection area, in square metres, added to the junction beyond the basic cross-roads area.

K = a factor depending on site conditions, but inevitably less than 100, which is the figure for ideal conditions.

Peak-hour K values, are approximately:

3-way junction	64 pcu/h/m
4-way junction	56 pcu/h/m
5- or more -way junctions	52 pcu/h/m

Further details of the research leading to the development of the new-layout roundabouts are available in TRRL Report LR 356, *Capacity of single-level intersections* by F C Blackmore.

A mini roundabout may be of any diameter greater than 1 metre but the smallest sizes are best used only at 3-way junctions. More suitable at most locations are roundabouts of 4 to 8 metres in diameter, the actual size being usually one third of the diameter of a circle inscribed within the outer carriageway boundaries. It is of fundamental importance that the approaches to the roundabout are widened and traffic deflected away from a straight-through movement. Where possible, within the available junction space, flared approaches of 1 in 1 to 1 in 5 are desirable, and angled islands, studs or painted lines should be used to ensure deflection into a multi-lane 'Give Way' line.

Traffic signals too will, in appropriate locations, reduce overall delays and increase throughput. Provided that total junction traffic exceeds 1200 vehicles per hour, (or 800 vehicles per hour on a site with poor visibility) the delays are likely to be reduced. But the reduction of delays and the relief of congestion are not the only possible reasons for installation of automatic traffic signals. At accident black spots, at heavily pedestrian-trafficked junctions, at extremely hazardous or delay-causing side-road entries, and at junctions regularly controlled by police, then significantly lower traffic flows can be accepted as justifying signals. The system-wide delays will probably be increased but the overall advantages to the community may well outweigh this specific vehicle-user disbenefit.

Traffic Signal Justification

The Department of the Environment's Technical Memorandum H1/73 of 6 Jan 1973, specifies the *reduced* traffic flows (below the 'normal' 1200 veh/h) which merit consideration being given to the installation of automatic traffic signals at junctions when — and only when — at least two other justifications for signalization are present. These are:

Location	Total junction traffic flows* vehicles/hour
Large urban area	500
Suburban and small urban area	400
Elsewhere	300

* At least 30% of total junction flows must enter by side road.

The hourly traffic flows used in these and other traffic-signal criteria are the average of the four busiest hours in any 24-hour period.

Linked Traffic Signals

Generally speaking, and particularly in the larger urban areas, the linking of automatic traffic signals will afford extra benefits over and above the benefits attributable to the sum of the individually controlled junctions. Around 10 per cent reduction in delays is a modest target. The biggest and best-known British examples of linked traffic signals, giving complete area traffic control (ATC), are those operating so successfully in West London and in Glasgow. Other important European ATC systems include the installations at Aachen, Madrid and Berlin.

But the advantages of linked signals or ATC are not restricted to the large city central areas. Significant benefits can be obtained from smaller installations, as long as the density of the proposed linked signals within the specified area is not less than 4 installations per square kilometre, or the spacing along a road is not less than 4 per kilometre. Signal systems of this type can be linked locally to master controllers or, utilizing spare capacity, handled by a remote computer. Where the above density/spacing criterion is met and a system of more than 30 linked signals is proposed, than a full ATC system can be initiated.

Resulting from research undertaken at the Glasgow and West London ATC systems, and in other locations, it is clear that the plans which control the operation of the linked signals can best be prepared on a fixed time basis. Fixed time systems are equally, or even more, effective and certainly cost less than the alternative, traffic-responsive systems. Fixed time systems also have the advantage of being simple in concept, implementation and operation.

The best-known fixed time systems at present available in Britain for the development of control plans are known as TRANSYT, COMBINATION, or SIGOP, in each of which the signal timing plans are derived by off-line computer operation from historical data. Once a series of basic plans has been developed for an overall system, these can be brought into operation and changed on a time and/or day basis, again established basically from the historical data. Within the scope of fixed time systems such as TRANSYT it is possible to bias the control plans to facilitate passage for certain types of vehicle — such as buses. It is also possible to arrange the control plan to decrease flows in environmental areas, diverting traffic out onto more acceptable routes — a facility capable of increasing use.

Pedestrianization Measures

Moving somewhat away from measures designed to improve the flow of traffic through towns, to consider now the improvement of the pedestrian environment, the closing of streets to all vehicular traffic is of course the ultimate approach; and there is much to be said for commencing the planning of any traffic management system by first designating the areas to be pedestrianized. The main problem associated with this approach in existing urban areas is that of access to the properties affected by the street closure. Pedestrianization in new developments is not, by our definition, traffic management but more appropriate to longer-range transport planning. If the area devoted to pedestrians is not large then the access/servicing problem is at least minimized, but in larger pedestrianized areas it may be more appropriate to permit limited vehicle entry.

As in other traffic-management measures, it is important to ensure that the measure itself, i.e. the pedestrianization, while improving the environment within its own boundaries, does not at the same time cause environmental problems in nearby streets due to the diverted traffic.

It is important too, in planning pedestrianized areas, to allow for vehicle access for the pedestrians themselves. This sounds over-simple but sometimes parking and access measures are provided for car-users without similar facilities for bus passengers. Where practical, bus services should be routed to pass by the boundaries of the pedestrian areas and/or on roads which cross longer pedestrian ways. Sometimes it may be appropriate to permit bus operation through the pedestrianized area itself, but the potential dangers to pedestrians of this move should not be overlooked.

Where bus operation and/or limited vehicle access (for delivery) is permitted within pedestrian areas, the roadway must be clearly defined, by kerbs etc., thereby precluding overall decorative-slab paving and the like. The width of carriageway provided for bus, and when permitted, service vehicle, access should be the minimum safe passing width, and the layout of the road should be such as physically to deter movement at other than a low speed. A speed limit alone is seldom if ever appropriate or workable.

Bus Priority Measures

Bus operation and bus travel generally can be improved in the short term by traffic management measures such as with- and contra-flow bus lanes within the limits of the existing carriageway. These measures are dealt with in greater detail in the chapter on Public Transport, for they have a place of their own in comprehensive long-term transport planning. With-flow lanes particularly, however, are a (relatively) readily applied short-term measure which in appropriate circumstances can provide considerable benefits.

Lorry Routes

Finally, in this brief review of traffic management techniques/measures, one which is frequently overlooked because of its greater impact on rural roads, not normally considered for traffic management — the designation of specific routes for heavy lorries. On a national scale this is already in hand, but similar principles can be applied to lesser areas — once the requirements are defined.

It is not always necessary to designate urban roads specifically for heavy lorries. The same effect can often be attained by signposting and making the alternative routes less attractive — by banning turns, judicious one-way operations, etc. A prerequisite of any such lorry restrictions/routeing, in both urban and rural areas, however, is the definition of a road hierarchy. Where should the lorries go and where should they not go? Where must they go? Once the lorry routes are defined it is possible to initiate minor improvements, such as easing bends, to make them more attractive to the lorry driver.

The other rural problem amenable to traffic management measures is that of the leisure driver. National Parks and other scenic areas attract increasing numbers of people, usually by car. There is normally no case for considering restricting the use of the private car for this purpose, or for diverting trips to public transport. There is therefore a need to provide facilities for the car. This means, among other things, adequate car parks (perhaps perforated concrete with grass inserts to preserve a green appearance), adequate signposting to the point of attraction — from well afield — and adequate lane marking at the actual location, where traffic is heaviest. Equally, unless attractive picnic spots are provided, and properly equipped, the public will make their own — at the expense of the verges, etc.

Implementation of Traffic-Management Measures

Although, of necessity, we have reviewed several of the available traffic-management measures individually and in isolation, their implementation should always, in common with other aspects of transportation planning, be on an integrated, comprehensive basis. An overall short-term plan should be developed, taking full account of the likely environmental consequences, and as far as possible its effects evaluated.

Normal evaluation procedures, such as described later in this book for urban systems or for individual inter-urban schemes, are not readily applied to traffic-management measures. These are commonly assessed merely by on-the-ground trial implementation, in which case, before-and-after studies are of particular importance in order to assess effectiveness. Some traffic-management measures however can, in an admittedly limited way, be pre-evaluated on economic grounds. For example, this could be undertaken by assessing the annual number of personal injury accidents prevented and valuing these at £1400 each in urban areas or £2300 each in rural areas. Note — These values, from

TRRL Report LR 396, are at 1970 prices. The *real* cost increase per year is usually taken as 3 per cent per annum. Delay time caused or saved is usually costed at £1 per vehicle-hour.

Appraisal of Measures for Accident Reduction

Example: A road carrying 800 veh/h (peak 4-hour average) and crossed by 500 ped/h, with an accident record of 5 pi accidents per year has a Zebra crossing planned.

$$\text{Accident benefits} = 5 \times 0.5 \times £1400 = £3500 \text{ per year}$$
$$\text{(50\% of present 5 accidents per year)}$$

Vehicle delays

$$= 0.5 \text{ sec (per 100 ped/h)} \times 500/100 \times 800 \text{ veh/h}$$
$$\times 12 \text{ h} \times 365/3600 \times £1$$

$$= £2400 \text{ per year}$$

Cost of installing Zebra crossing, say £500

$$\text{Rate of return} = £3500 - £2400/£500 = 220\%$$

Note — Appendix II to the Dept. of the Environment's Circular Roads 21/68 affirms that Zebra crossings reduce accidents by approximately 50 per cent and delay to vehicles caused by Zebras is approximately 0.5 sec per 100 ped/h.

Evaluation aside, it is essential when implementing, or planning the implementation of a programme of traffic-management measures to ensure that the public and the police etc. are fully able to understand the requirements. It is all too easy to initiate some new management measure which the public are not able quickly to comprehend, with chaos resulting almost immediately. With careful planning and advance warnings, this can usually be avoided.

Finally, when planning urban traffic-management measures as a short-term programme, it is important to ensure that they neither preclude nor pre-empt without adequate justification, the later implementation of the more comprehensive, and inevitably more expensive, medium-term measures.

SUMMARY

a) The major role of traffic management in comprehensive transport planning is to obtain the optimum short-term use of existing urban transport facilities at largely insignificant cost, in advance of comprehensive medium-term measures being implemented. But traffic management measures also have a not insignificant role in the medium-term plan.

b) As always, information is the prime requirement in advance of traffic-management planning. Surveys for the medium-term plan should be used to serve both purposes.

c) Available traffic-management measures range from the well-known traffic engineering techniques, through pedestrian safety measures and parking controls (for the purpose of easing through-flow) to single and linked junction controls, and on to the more far-reaching bus priority measures, more appropriate to the medium-term plan.

d) Traffic-management measures should be flexible enough to adapt to changing demands and conditions.

e) ATC can produce a 10 per cent reduction in overall delay time over a wide area. Improved roundabouts (Minis) can increase the capacity of a junction by 25 per cent. Pelican crossings can be expected to reduce accidents by 60 per cent compared with a Zebra crossing, which in turn should reduce accidents by about 50 per cent over no crossing. At £1 per vehicle hour delay time and £1400 per urban personal injury accident, these improvements offer significant economic benefits.

f) In rural areas, measures akin to urban traffic-management measures are appropriate at leisure attractors.

g) Care should be taken in implementing traffic-management measures to ensure that their implementation does not cause chaos.

5

Parking

The average private car is actually in motion for only about 400 hours a year. For the remaining 8360 hours in each year it is stationary — parked. And although for considerably more than half of that stationary time the car will probably be at the owner's home garage, it may well be parked away from home for 2000 hours a year. In 1971 there were fifteen-and-a-half million vehicles using the roads of Britain, which means a parking problem of some thirty thousand million (3×10^{10}) vehicle-parking-hours. Clearly the parked vehicle is a major matter for consideration. £29 million a year (gross) was spent by local authorities alone in catering for it in the early 1970s.

Consider then the places where vehicles are parked, other than at home. They are:

a) On street
    i) in residential areas
    ii) in central areas without control
    iii) in central areas with control

b) Off street
    i) in publicly operated, publicly available parks
    ii) in privately operated, publicly available parks
    iii) in private parks.

We have already seen, in Figure 4.1, how just a few parked vehicles on a public road can seriously reduce the capacity of that road. It is also appropriate to consider the road-space cost of on-street parking, which is often forgotten. It would not be at all unusual for a new, single-carriageway road in a town centre to cost about £1.5 million per kilometre, including land costs. At this cost, each parking bay, together with the space alienated by it, costs more than £3000. To recover a notional 10 per cent return on this road-space capital investment alone, each bay should earn at least 10p per hour.* And this ignores such considerations as the cost of collection of this revenue and the possibility of occasional empty spaces — it is merely the cost of the road space. How many meter bays are charged for even at this minimum rate?

Admittedly, many of the town-centre roads where parking is permitted will not have cost £1½ million per kilometre to build, but it is partly the congestion caused by their use which is generating demands for relief roads at present-day prices. It is surely only reasonable therefore that existing space used for parking be equated with replacement/relief prices.

* Basis of the cost per hour is:
One kilometre of 7.30m wide road at £1.5m per km (£2½m/mile of 24' road)
Parking bay plus manoeuvring and unused space = 2.25m × 7.5m
Capital cost per bay = £1 500 000 × 2.25/7.30 × 7.5/1000 = £3400 per bay
At 10%, £340 income per annum is needed
Utilization, say 300 days per annum, 10 hours per day
Hence, minimum charge is in excess of 10p per hour.

Residential Parking

Because of the ever-increasing volume of traffic on our roads, and the congestive effect of parked cars, there is a clear need for some form of central-area parking policy almost everywhere. The need for control of parking in residential streets is less certain. There is undoubtedly considerable environmental disbenefit in the sight of a quiet residential street with parked cars lining the kerbs. Against this however is the likely reduction in speed of passing traffic with the associated improvement in the residents' safety. In outer suburbs and in new residential estates, adequate off-street, within-curtelage parking and/or garage space will customarily be provided and the residual on-street parking problem is negligible.

Closer to town centres and in older residential streets, adequate off-street space may not have been provided, nor now be available. In such areas, on-street parking reserved for residents may be the answer — or a policy of *laissez faire*, depending on closeness to the central area and the likely demand for parking space. In residential areas adjacent to the town centre however, the parking must be controlled if any central transportation planning is to be effective. The control can be by free resident parking — with cars displaying a resident's badge — or by fee-paying resident-reserved spaces using such systems as the De La Rue daily-stamp-fee card, which has been adopted in the City of Westminster.

Central-area, On-street, Uncontrolled Parking

Although it may seem unbelievable to the city motorist accustomed to hunting for a vacant meter bay, there are still many towns in Britain with uncontrolled or virtually uncontrolled parking in or very near to the central area. At the very least, however, it has long been incumbent on authorities to indicate the *manner* in which vehicles should park. Basically, the alternatives are:
a) parallel to and alongside the kerb,
b) at right-angles to and adjacent to the kerb,
c) diagonally onto the kerb,
d) centrally in wide road, at right-angles or diagonally.

Inevitably, with most urban roads being relatively narrow, most parking in Britain is kerbside-parallel. Parking at right-angles to the kerb is of course capable of accommodating more vehicles per running kilometre but is usually only practicable where a space behind the general kerb-line can be paved.

Diagonal parking too is uncommon but is also capable of accommodating more vehicles per running kilometre — at a corresponding loss of road width. Drive-in diagonal parking is undoubtedly more convenient for the motorist. An American study some years ago timed cars *backing out* of diagonal parking in an average of 12 seconds (driving in of course being quicker still) compared with 32 seconds to *back into* a parallel-to-the-kerb bay. Generally however, both right-angle and diagonal parking are around twice as liable to cause accidents as is parallel parking. Of equal importance, the road space taken up for the manoeuvring out of a diagonal or right-angle parking bay is considerably greater than that for a kerb-side parallel bay.

The same considerable disadvantages apply to road-centre parking — with the added problem of emerging into the fast stream — and the shortage of suitable wide streets in urban Britain. The vast majority of on-street parking in Britain is therefore, rightly, parallel to and alongside the kerb.

Central-area On-street Controlled Parking

For all the continued existence of uncontrolled central-area on-street parking in some towns, some form of control is inevitably proving necessary, even in the quietest and best-planned of towns, to cope with the ever-increasing demand. There are three standard and well-known methods of control available to the transport planner:

a) time restriction (20 minutes in any hour, etc.)
b) disc parking
c) parking meters.

The characteristics, advantages, disadvantages and economics of these methods can be summarized in tabular form:

Aspect	Time restriction	Disc	Meter
Control (Wages)	Warden (£25+ weekly)	Warden (£25+ weekly)	Warden (£25+ weekly)
Cost of implementation	Negligible (signs only)	Negligible (signs only)	Approximately £40 per bay
Revenue	Nil	Nil (possibility of advert. revenue)	2½p–10p per hour in central areas (1974)
Economics	Net loss (borne by ratepayer, not by motorist)	Net loss (borne by ratepayer, not by motorist)	Possible small surplus (no charge on rates — costs met by motorists)
Ease of supervision	Dependent on warden recording arrival & departure times — no proof. Difficult to control well.	Relatively easy — warden merely checks disc set correctly.	Easy — visual indication by flag of time-expiry and penalty (check for meter-feeding).
Flexibility	Needs complicated notices to vary restrictions by time of day.	Easy — disc can indicate different periods at different times.	NIL (Pay or no-pay option) Hourly charges can be increased as costs rise or as deterrent.
Environmental effect on streetscape	Negligible (signs)	Negligible (signs)	Unsightly ('forest' of meters)
Other characteristics	Can include provision for resident parking.	Strangers to town will not have disc on arrival. Because no need for marked bays, can accommodate more cars than meter control.	Problems of availability of correct coinage; vandalism and theft.

The difficulties of adequate control and the financial loss inherent in the time-restriction method means that its use is declining in most towns. Disc parking, since 1957 the only method in use in central

Paris, against the continuing advice of the Prefect, who favoured the introduction of meters, and whose advice has now been taken, has in more recent years been adopted in such English towns as Cheltenham, Devizes, Harrogate and Oxford. It too has the disadvantage of its deficit operation, which is only occasionally outweighed by the environmental case, as in the towns mentioned. The most important method of on-street parking control is likely to remain the meter — at least until some form of road-use pricing mechanism can be perfected. But as recently as 1970 there were still only 36 towns in Britain using meter control, although admittedly these included all the towns with populations of 400 000 or more.

Parking Meters

It has been suggested, and it is generally accepted, that the optimum average occupancy of metered parking bays should be 85 per cent, i.e. 15 per cent of parking bays will be empty, available for the arriving motorist. As parking demand varies throughout the day, the parking fee is determined so as to give the 85 per cent occupancy during the hours of maximum demand — from around 11 a.m. until the early afternoon. Seldom if ever is the parking charge determined on the basis of the cost of the road space lost to other users. Just the cost of providing the meter and enforcing its use is of the order of 2½p per bay per hour, which is still (in 1974) a common fee in many smaller towns.

Cost of Parking Meters

Assume meter costs £40 which cost is written off over 4 years. Assume a ratio of one warden to 25 bays and a warden's pay as £1250 per year. Meter is in use 10 hours per day, 310 days per year.

Then
Meter cost	£10 p.a.	
Warden's wages	£50 p.a.	
Overheads, say	£10 p.a.	
Total per bay	£70 p.a.	

$$= 70/310 \times 100/10 = 2\frac{1}{2}\text{p/h}$$

If ratio is one warden to 100 bays, then costs fall to £32 p.a. or approximately 1p/h.

One reason for the size of this operating cost is the ratio of metered bays to traffic wardens. In central London this can be as low as 22 meters per warden — which level is in part due to the effective use of graduated charges. After two hours at most meters, an excess charge of either 10 or twenty times the hourly charge is levied for an extension of half an hour. Beyond the extension period, a fixed fine is imposed — effectively again a further excess charge. By contrast, in San Francisco, where no excess charges are imposed, there is one warden to 108 metered bays, at a correspondingly lower cost per bay.

Irrespective of their economic sense, parking meters offer the best currently available control of on-street parking. Their present under-utilized facility of increasing charges can ensure that space is always available for the would-be short-term parker. There is a considerable school of thought that advocates the abolition of the normal 2-hour limit plus excess charge and its replacement by a no-time-limit availability at an appropriate deterrent cost. This would certainly make supervision and enforcement simpler, and as we shall see later, these are the major problem areas in meter parking.

Off-street Parking

No matter by what method, or how well it is controlled, on-street parking takes up road space that is better used for movement. Clearly, in order to reduce, or at least contain, the increasing traffic congestion it is better that vehicles should be parked elsewhere — off-street. And the two obvious forms of off-street park are:
a) surface parks
b) multi-storey parks.

The greatest demand for parking facilities and the greatest need for them to be off-street rather than on-street, is in central areas — where land costs are highest. Permanent surface car parks in central areas are therefore likely to be uneconomic — dependent on the standard of construction, the capital cost could be as high as for on-street parking. The most common central-area surface car parks are therefore transitory, inter-development sites where economic considerations are of less importance. Surface parks are more appropriate slightly further out from the central area, where land costs will be less for instance at 'park-and-ride' locations — see below.

In central areas then, multi-storey car parks are usually the most appropriate form of provision. Subject to the actual demand, it is generally agreed that five floors and a total capacity of 500 to 750 cars is about the optimum size for a central area park, although there may well be local justification for exceeding these figures. Parkers dislike excessively long drives or walks within the confines of the park — hence the five-floor optimum. The capacity limitation is a function of the time needed to locate a car and leave the park, and the capacity of the adjacent road system for rapid absorption of the exiting vehicles.

Although multi-storey car parks can be organized for attendants to park the vehicles, this is not popular with drivers, who obviously prefer to retain their keys and to have access directly to the car while parked. Customer-parking however imposes a requirement for more generous parking bays, access aisles and ramps, which is to some extent counter-balanced by the need for larger reservoir space in attendant-parking facilities.

Clearly the cost of multi-storey car parks will vary considerably with the location and the prevailing land costs. In 1970 a survey of costs of 21 concrete-construction multi-storey parks showed an average construction cost per space of £400 (within a range from £295 to £1110 per space). Allowing for central area land costs of £½ million or more per acre, the total cost per parking space will easily amount to £1000. At that cost, and allowing for both annual operating costs and capital charges, a break-even cost per bay of 5p per hour is not at all un-reasonable.

Determination of Break-even Costs per Parking Bay

a) Assume the not unreasonable requirement of a ten per cent return on capital — hence £100 p.a. per bay.

b) The wages element of the annual operating costs for a 500-car park might well be based on two pairs of cashier/attendants and a handyman/cleaner plus health insurance charges etc. totalling £140 per week, or £7000 p.a. Translated into costs per bay this is £14 p.a.

c) An allowance needs to be made for local authority rates (irrespective of whether or not the park is owned or operated by the authority). An analysis of 26 car parks in 1971/2 indicated a range of actual rates payable per bay varying from £5 to £20, with an average of just under £11 p.a.

d) An allowance for building maintenance, and equipment maintenance and depreciation, together with electricity, water and other services of £7 p.a., and for general administrative and other overhead charges of £6 p.a. should also be allowed.

In summary therefore, annual costs to be recouped might well be of the order of:

Capital charges (a)	£100
Wages etc. (b)	£ 14
Rates (c)	£ 11
Maintenance & services (d)	£ 7
Administration & overheads (d)	£ 6
	£138 p.a. (at 1972 levels of cost)

At 310 days a year, 9 hours per day (say 2800 hours per year) and ignoring the virtual certainty of empty bays at some time during the year the hourly break-even cost per bay is thus:

$$13\,800/2800 = 4.9\text{p } say\,5\text{p/h}$$

In fact, 80 per cent utilization would be considered good on a year-round basis.

Note

1. The costs quoted are notional ones but generally realistic in terms of 1972 costs, and serve to highlight the importance of the wages and rates elements. They also make no allowance for commercial profit or surplus.

2. These figures are derived from those quoted by H. Selwyn Lewis in his paper *Projecting profitability of car parks* at the 1972 BPA Seminar, *Making Parking Pay.*

Many authorities have in the past been unwilling to levy an economic parking charge, particularly when land costs are less obviously high. In these conditions the motorist may well have alternative parking possibilities — the authorities may either opt for a purely nominal charge, or lease the car park facilities to a commercial operator at a rent related solely to structural costs, excluding the land cost. The local authorities make good their parking deficit from the Rate fund or from any surplus from meter operations. Commercial parking operators however, other than those operating in property let at subsidized rents, cannot afford to do other than charge the full economic rate and make a profit, if they are to remain in business. There is thus, at present, often the anomalous situation of desirable commercial car-parking operations being impossible due to subsidized competition from local authority facilities, both on- and off-street.

A first essential in planning for parking control — should commercial operation be an objective — is clearly to ensure that all parking facilities are costed on a true economic or commercial basis. This entails abolishing any subsidization of parking costs from local authority funds. At the same time, as no off-street parking facility can operate commercially alongside uncontrolled on-street parking opportunities, the presence of a well-enforced meter system is essential.

But car parks do not usually charge a flat rate per hour as we have calculated above. A typical tariff might be:

$$
\begin{array}{lll}
0 - & 2 \text{ hours} & 10\text{p} \\
2 - & 4 \text{ hours} & 20\text{p} \\
4 - & 6 \text{ hours} & 25\text{p} \\
6 - & 9 \text{ hours} & 40\text{p} \\
9 - & 12 \text{ hours} & 50\text{p} \\
12 - & 24 \text{ hours} & 60\text{p}
\end{array}
$$

Although the rate per hour upon which this tariff is based is clearly 5p per hour for the first five hours and a little over 4p/hour thereafter, this is not the hourly rate which is effectively received. Figure 5.1 shows clearly how a parker staying for, say, 2½ hours actually pays 8p/hour. And J. M. Thompson, in a survey of London parking durations, showed that, as is intuitively fairly obvious, for other-than-commuter parkers, something like 78 per cent of parkers stay less than 3 hours. To determine the estimated revenue from a car park therefore, there is clearly a need for a fairly accurate duration survey.

The Objectives of Parking Controls

So far we have considered only the simple, elementary and commercially-oriented aspects of parking control. Some years ago, Messrs. Roth and Thompson suggested that the reasons for and objectives of parking control were:

to prevent obstruction to moving vehicles,

to reduce accidents,

to make effective use of parking space,

to preserve amenity, notably in towns of great historical value,

to act as a restraint mechanism for the use of roads in congested areas. Today, there can be no doubt whatsoever that parking control has also to be considered in the broader context of overall transportation planning. Other than physical restrictions on road space (bus lanes, etc.) it is, at present, the only method of travel restraint which is available to the planner in his aim of providing a balanced, comprehensive and integrated transportation system.

In the past, parking control has been applied mainly to reduce congestion on the roads, to enable the roads to better handle the traffic demand, by getting the parked cars off the road into off-street parks. Today, parking control is used to influence the actual urban demand — to deter people from making the trip at all by car — to divert the trip onto the public-transport alternative. But at present there is no universal need to deter all car trips (although this need may arise in some localities) but only those who do not need their car. And that means the commuter. The person who drives to work, with a vehicle occupancy of around 1½ persons/car, parks the car for the day and drives home again at night should be discouraged. There is far less

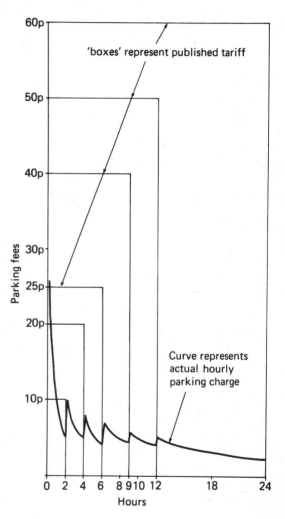

Fig. 5.1 A notional parking tariff graphed by time to indicate effective hourly rates

need, if any, to deter the shopping motorist who tends to avoid the peak periods and to park for shorter periods, permitting multiple use of the same parking space.

There is also of course considerable disadvantage in deterring car-borne shoppers, who might divert their trade to out-of-town shopping centres with a consequent withering away of the traditional town centre. The possible modal change of work trips however is unlikely to detract from the viability of the town centre or the factory area. One of the aims of an urban parking policy could therefore be to encourage the short-term shopping parker and to deter the long-term commuter parker. The more fundamental aim today must inevitably be to balance the *total travel* demand with the available *and acceptable* capacity of the achievable future transport system. Note that there is no question of preventing trips, merely ensuring that they are made by the most suitable mode and that this enforced transference is only applied to the limit of what the public will accept in terms of environmental effects.

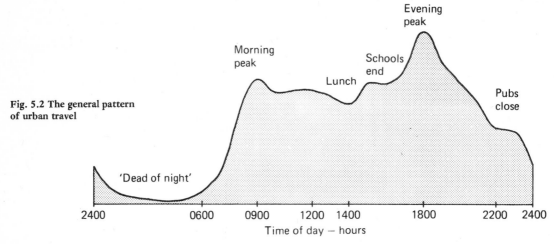

Fig. 5.2 The general pattern of urban travel

Parking Restraint Measures

How then can town-centre parking be controlled to effect these requirements? There are basically three available methods:

control by price

control by limitation of space

control by opening times.

Each of these methods on its own has its disadvantages and problems; control by price is less than 100 per cent effective where firms pay employees' parking charges; limitation of space implies a first-come-first-served policy, which is the opposite of control; control by time may unintentionally deter the early shopper. Parking restraint is therefore usually applied by a combination of these measures adjusted to individual urban circumstances.

It is possible to arrange a parking tariff so as to deter the long-term parker, yet to not deter the short-term user — something like:

$$
\begin{array}{lll}
0 - & 2 \text{ hours} & 10p \\
2 - & 4 \text{ hours} & 20p \\
4 - & 6 \text{ hours} & 40p \\
6 - & 9 \text{ hours} & 75p \\
9 - & 24 \text{ hours} & 80p \\
\end{array}
$$

Together with this sort of approach, it is essential that the sale of cheap-rate parking season tickets to regular long-term parkers be abolished, as this is a total negation of the aims of deterring commuter parkers.

Limitation of space will have an effect on the price tariff, in that if there is a nascent demand for, say, 1000 spaces but a provision of only 500, then the price will help to deter the effective queue. Although there may not in practice be a queue there will be economic competition for the available spaces.

As most workers need to be at work by, say, 0930 at the latest, any car park which does not open for business until after that time imposes an extremely effective restraint on the commuter parker. Clearly though, this form of restraint cannot be adopted at every car park within a central area – there are some people who have legitimate reasons for arriving early at a park.

Enforcement

But all of these parking control restraint measures depend on control of the parking facilities by the planning authorities. And this is of course the major problem in parking control. In many towns, developers having throughout the 1950s and 1960s been encouraged by the planning authorities to provide firm's parks, as many as 50 per cent of the available parking spaces are privately owned for private use. A further proportion of the parking spaces, although publicly-available are privately owned and/or operated. At present the available legislation does not permit the local planning authorities to impose any sort of control on these parking spaces. Future parking provision can of course be controlled – instead of requiring not less than x parking spaces per 100 employees or per $10m^2$ of floor area, as in the past, the requirement could be not *more* than x spaces.

One solution to the problem of private parking spaces which is often canvassed – and is probably the most practical solution – is some form of differential rating of available or possible parking space in excess of a very small amount. Exemption to the parking rate could be afforded the owner who could demonstrate that he had so arranged the layout of his site as to preclude its use for parking. The other solution to the problem of private parking space is of course national legislation to bring all off-street parking facilities under control by licensing by the local transport planning authority, as has indeed been suggested.

But off-street parking facilities are not the only ones with problems in enforcing parking policies and control. Enforcement is also a major problem with meter control. In London as long ago as 1969 there was between a 15 per cent and a 20 per cent chance of escaping without excess charge, fine or prosecution for meter offences. The present situation is unlikely, as yet, to be better, until owner liability is enforceable. The prevention of meter-feeding too is now known to be largely unenforceable.

Bearing in mind that until owner liability is authorized there is virtually no *economic* logic in trying to locate and prosecute parking offenders, two fundamentally different approaches to on-street parking enforcement are:
a) removal of offending vehicle, by driving or lifting away to car pound,
b) rendering vehicle immobile.
The advantages of physical removal are of course that congestion is immediately reduced and the offending driver is put to trouble to reclaim his car. Disadvantages of course are the staff and/or lifting equipment needed to operate the removal system.

Immobilizing the vehicle has not, to the writer's knowledge, been used in Britain, but in America and in Paris, what is known as 'the Denver shoe' has been used effectively. A large lump of iron is locked to a wheel of the offending car which is only removed, after deliberate delays, on payment of a fine. The advantages of this system are the absolute effectiveness of the deterrent and the relatively few staff and little equipment needed to operate it. The great disadvantage is that the congestive obstruction of the offence is compounded rather than alleviated — but against that, the deterrent is so effective that over a period of time offenders decrease.

But irrespective of precisely how on-street parking control is implemented, there can be no doubt at all that effective enforcement there must be. Without effective enforcement any form of control of off-street spaces must fail, and with it a keystone of the whole transportation policy.

With parking under control and its availability deliberately restricted, there will be a change of mode for some journeys. The modal change may not be very great but whatever its size the demand for bus services will increase and must be met. The 'stick' will have been applied; there is then need for the 'carrot' of *better* public transport services, i.e. improvement in regularity, reliability, journey speeds, comfort, etc., as has already been suggested.

Park-and-Ride

Over the last few years there has been a noticeable trend for housing areas to spread out, on the outskirts of towns, rather than to cluster in high-density areas. This residential dispersal is the opposite of a public transport service planner's ideal and is a positive encouragement to the use of the private car for commuting. The disadvantages of the dispersed layout for public transport operations and the application of restraint on the use of the car for commuting therefore appear to conflict with each other. There is a compromise position, however, which is increasingly popular in America and may well be appropriate in the larger towns in Britain (and certainly so for London). This is the park-and-ride system.

Park-and-ride is a combination of travel modes whereby a commuter drives his car from his home to some convenient collection point where he parks it. He then transfers to some form of public transport to complete his journey to the more congested town centre. On the return journey the process is of course reversed. Although housing has dispersed, employment areas have not, to any great extent, and it is operationally practicable to provide public transport to these areas. A parking-space-saving derivative from park-and-ride is the appropriately named 'kiss-and-ride' in which system the husband is driven to the public transport interchange by his wife, bids her a fond farewell and completes his journey by public transport. The wife then has the use of the car for the rest of the day before meeting her husband on his return journey.

Clearly, the effective operation of a park-and-ride service will depend on several considerations:

a) adequate parking facilities must be available at the interchange, at low or nil charge to the regular user,

b) the waiting time for the public transport connection must be kept to a minimum, and if at all possible, under-cover waiting facilities should be provided,

c) there should be an adequate 'market' — i.e. a large catchment area of low residential density,

d) the overall travel time,* house to office or factory, should be comparable to that by car,

e) the overall travel cost,* house to work-place, should preferably be less than, or at very least, equal to that by car,

f) availability of parking spaces near to the central destination should be severely restricted.

Associated with the overall travel time and cost considerations mentioned above is the actual length of the journey. A short overall journey situation (such as in a smaller town) will not be appropriate for the successful operation of a park-and-ride system, because of the increased relative importance of the interchange delay time. Savings in time and cost were the most important reasons for favouring a park-and-ride facility quoted by commuters in 1968 at Stuttgart in Germany. Similarly, avoidance of high central area parking costs was a major reason for Washington DC commuters favouring a park-and-ride facility in America.

The determination of the size of a park-and-ride park will be dependent on many of the considerations mentioned above, but also on the average household income and car ownership levels within the catchment area. This is reflected too in the residential density mentioned above. In this respect, the car-demand ratio — the number of driving licences in a household divided by the number of cars in the household — is an important factor. Given an area of one-car households with an average car-demand ratio of 2 or more, then the interchange is likely to attract 'kiss-and-ride' patronage. With more than one car per household (most frequently found in low-density housing areas) then park-and-ride will be most likely to be adopted. Although parking space need be less for a 'kiss-and-ride' facility, adequate, carefully planned space must nevertheless be provided for the drop-off/pick-up area.

And, extending this consideration of parking space requirements, it should be appreciated that, in larger towns subject to restraint by parking control, the established methods of calculation of space needs are no longer appropriate, except perhaps as an upper limit. Parking space requirements will usually best be determined in the context of a detailed transportation study of the urban area.

Outside the larger urban areas however, in small towns and at out-of-town hypermarkets and the like, the use of generalized parking needs criteria remains appropriate. The author's suggestions for preliminary use are:

Retail shops 1 space per 20 m² retail floor space
(assuming 50% of customers are car-borne†)

Restuarants, theatres 1 space per 3 seats
cinemas etc.

Sports stadia 1 space per 10 spectators

Outside urban central areas, there is a further requirement to be taken account of in comprehensive transport planning — lorry parks. A Government working party recommended in 1971 that a national network of 50 lorry parks be set up in Britain, each accommodating up to 300 heavy lorries, and this recommendation was adopted. A

* Note — It has been found that the public assessment of the cost of *waiting* time is about double that of travel time — no matter if the actual travel time be slow. A reliable, regular but slow public transport service is therefore preferable to an unreliable, irregular, faster one.

† For out-of-town shopping centres where nearer 100 per cent of customers are likely to be car-borne, this space requirement might well be doubled — to 1 space per 10 m².

national network of such parks for the long-distance lorry is planned
by the Department of the Environment. It is, of course, open to local
authorities to provide similar facilities for heavy vehicles operating
more locally. They will also need to back up these lorry park
facilities by introducing tough parking restrictions to prevent lorries
from continuing to park overnight etc. on urban streets.

Sites for Lorry Parks Should be:

a) in or near areas zoned for industry, away from residential areas,
b) on the outskirts of urban areas and convenient for bus services to
   town centres,
c) conveniently accessible to the lorry route system, with adequate
   minor access roads,
d) capable of accommodating a minimum of 100 lorries and a maximum
   of 300,
e) capable of being made secure, possibly with additional special
   security areas,
f) developed to provide suitable overnight accommodation for drivers,
   including recreational facilities.

Other Forms of Restraint

We have already dealt with parking control generally as a form of
restraint on certain types of journey. Other means of restraint are
possible, including of course, physical measures to restrict the use of
road space. More sophisticated but theoretically possible methods are
already being studied by the Department of the Environment and the
Greater London Council. Methods under investigation include supplementary licensing, toll charges and electronic metering systems (road
pricing). The first two methods have the disadvantage of needing a
series of control entry points around a cordon for licence inspection,
and temporary-licence issue or toll collection. The staff needed for
either of these systems is considerable, as would be the cost of
physically providing gates etc. for entry control. Against this, the
benefits in terms of reduced congestion and associated environmental
improvements can be considerable.

Electronic metering appears to have theoretical advantages, but
it suffers from the major practical disadvantage that to operate the
system it would be necessary for most vehicles to be fitted with the
metering device, the 'black box'. It is unlikely therefore that a road-
pricing restraint system can be operated in the near future.

Research is continuing on the alternative restraint methods, but
in the context of a medium-term plan, the control of parking, together
with related traffic-management measures, must currently remain the
prime measure available to transportation planners.

SUMMARY

a) The average private car spends considerably more time parked away from home than it does in motion.

b) Parking can be on- or off-street — both types need to be controlled.

c) On-street parking can best be controlled by parking meter, but the charges need to be realistic, bearing in mind the cost of the road space neutralized by the parked car.

d) Off-street parking needs to be charged for at an economic rate, without subsidy from parking-meter revenue or from the General Rate Fund.

e) Parking control should be directed at balancing the travel demand with the acceptable capacity of the transportation system as a whole — controlling by price and availability.

f) To be effective as a means of restraint, parking control must be enforced, which is easier said than done.

g) Park-and-ride, in suitable larger urban areas, may be an appropriate compromise between the flexibility of private car collection and the efficiency of public transport line haul — but it is unlikely to be effective in towns of less than, say, 200 000 population.

h) Other methods of travel restraint are possible in the long term, but other than physical space restrictions, parking control is the only means as yet available for use.

6

Urban Transportation Studies – Design and Surveys

So far we have looked at the overall problem of strategy development on a county-wide basis and examined some of the more major components from which these strategies are built up. We have briefly mentioned the need for special investigation of the larger urban areas, on an integrated basis, and the use of transportation study techniques in that process. We can now look at the urban transportation study in greater detail.

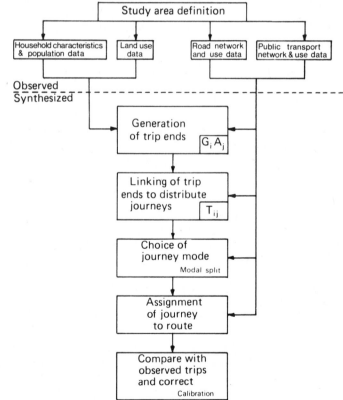

Fig. 6.1 The transportation study process — the upper part simplified

As we have already seen, a transportation study consists of the development of formulae, or models, enabling future travel demands to be forecast, and the assessment of alternative strategies for handling this demand, see Fig. 6.1. The model development which is central to the overall process depends, like nearly everything else in the field of transport planning, on the collection of data – by various surveys. Basically, these surveys are directed at the collection of data relevant to the uses of the land, the population and its trip-making characteristics and the components of the available transport system. Alongside and integrated with these surveys are those directed at obtaining information on present-day movements for comparing with predictions of these same movements.

Before any urban transportation study is commenced, however, a review of the urban transport situation must be instituted and the actual need for the study ascertained. Are there significant problems needing solution – or are the choices of future action so restricted that there is no need for the relatively sophisticated procedure of an urban transportation study?

The Study Area

Assuming the need for a study is confirmed, the next problem is to define the area to be studied. Administrative boundaries of urban areas, while undoubtedly convenient, will not necessarily be the most suitable for transportation study purposes. Ideally, the area to be studied should be fairly tight around an urban area, yet at the same time, including anticipated future growth areas within the boundary. Equally, the boundary should not be so tight that indecisive modelling of demand in areas around the boundary can significantly affect the present or future urban area demands. Nor should it be so close in to the urban areas that it is crossed by a large number of 'traffic-insignificant' roads, when slightly further out the number of boundary crossing points will be considerably reduced. With these conflicting requirements, clearly the study area boundary must to some extent, be a matter of subjective judgement.

The determination of the boundary of a study area should, where practicable, take account of natural or man-made movement-limitations – such as rivers, railway lines, motorways, etc., all of which require special facilities for crossing, and therefore form effective travel barriers. It is also of great importance to take account of the boundaries of other studies, both past, and projected for the near future. This is to enable future amalgamation and re-use of basic data, and, as far as possible, to ensure compatibility between adjacent studies. Finally, within the area design limitations already imposed, the boundary should, as far as possible, be so adjusted to cross radial roads at locations suitable for roadside surveys.

Another important point to watch is the avoidance of peninsulas and inlets. Peninsulas might be completely crossed by external traffic, which would thus be observed twice yet have virtually no effect on the internal area requirements. Inlets might well be crossed twice by internal traffic and at the same time, themselves form peninsulas nearby. Inlets too will cause confusion in balancing traffic flows, see Fig. 6.2.

To summarize then, the boundary, which will become the line of a cordon surrounding the urban transportation study area, should:

a) be 'sensibly' close around the urban development,
b) include potential development areas,
c) incorporate natural boundaries where possible and be compatible with other nearby studies,
d) avoid peninsulas and inlets,
e) be suitably located for roadside survey stations.

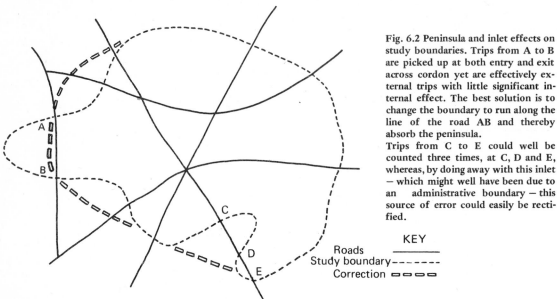

Fig. 6.2 Peninsula and inlet effects on study boundaries. Trips from A to B are picked up at both entry and exit across cordon yet are effectively external trips with little significant internal effect. The best solution is to change the boundary to run along the line of the road AB and thereby absorb the peninsula.

Trips from C to E could well be counted three times, at C, D and E, whereas, by doing away with this inlet — which might well have been due to an administrative boundary — this source of error could easily be rectified.

KEY
Roads ————
Study boundary - - - - - -
Correction ▭ ▭ ▭ ▭

Dividing the Study Area into Zones

The next stage in the study design is to divide up the study area into internal *zones* or small packets of land. These zones are usually smallest nearest the centre, increasing in size towards the boundary. This zonation is necessary in order to be able to handle and analyse the data which will be collected within the study area. The task of handling and analysing survey data by individual premises would be physically and financially almost impossible — some form of grouping is essential. Outside the study area the rest of the country too should be divided up into large external zones, which should also increase in size as they increase in distance from the study area.

Internal zones should be:

a) as internally homogeneous as possible — ideally a residential zone should contain only residential land use, but this is usually extremely difficult. In central areas particularly, shopping zones are often also office zones and usually contain an element of residential use. Hence 'as homogeneous *as possible*', i.e. a *preponderance* of one land use.

b) small enough to enable travel patterns to be reliably synthesized (intra-zonal trips cannot readily be modelled) yet large enough to ensure that the data collected within them is statistically significant. Population in residential zones is commonly within the range 1000 to 3000.

c) made up of one or more National Population Census Enumeration

Districts (EDs). This is important because the Census data which is of use in checking surveys etc. is available in terms of EDs – and they are almost always small enough to enable zones to be built on this basis. The only likely problem in the use of EDs for zonal definition is a large zone in an industrial area with a very low residential population.

d) amenable to the assembly of planning data – this may mean odd shapes to accommodate, say, a whole zone with a single planning use, but will save time and money when obtaining land use data for the study. It may also entail finer zoning in a fringe area earmarked for future development.

e) located with regard to major routes, natural, administrative, and study boundaries, adjacent study zone patterns etc. They should also be designed, as far as possible, to be equally appropriate to future land development. Each zone should be wholly within a single local authority area.

f) numbered in a logical sequence – logical, to enable checks to be made easily.

Relationship of Population to Numbers and Sizes of Zones

Examples of numbers of zones in recent urban transportation studies in Britain, related to study area population are:

Study area centred on	Population	Number of internal zones	Average popn. over all zones
Barnsley	91 000	72	1260
Gt. Yarmouth/Lowestoft	127 000	52	2450
Cambridge	144 000	90	1600
Slough	144 000	103	1400
Norwich	170 000	75	2280
Hull	345 000	153	2250
Doncaster	387 000	200	1930
Sheffield/Rotherham	730 000	430	1700

External zones may sometimes be sub-classified into intermediate and external zones. This subdivision is really only an acknowledgement that external zones adjacent to the study area – say within the surrounding sub-region or region – will need to be considerably smaller (finer zoning) than the true external zones comprising a remote but large part of the country. Both intermediate and true external zones should be compatible with adjacent studies' zonation, and also with the National zoning system, i.e., basically with local authority and other administrative boundaries.

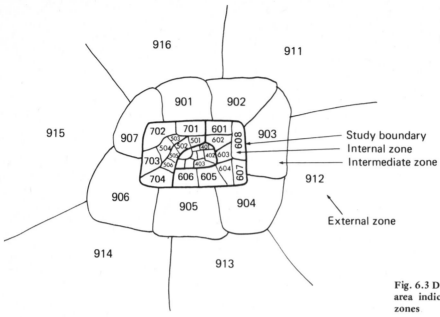

Fig. 6.3 Diagram of a notional study area indicating internal and external zones

Defining the Networks

Having now defined the study area and divided it up into easily handled groups of households and/or groups of trip attractions — work-places, shops, schools, etc. — we must next define the skeleton around which the study area and its component zones form the flesh — the road and public transport networks. Just as the survey area was defined and split into zones so the networks too need to be defined, broken down and codified.

It is not practicable to look at every stretch of road within the study area — obviously the traffic movements on a minor housing estate are of little significance in terms of overall urban transportation planning. So the roads of traffic significance — and those likely to attain significance in the future — are selected. It is customary, at this stage, to err on the generous side, including doubtfully significant roads, to be on the safe side. The selected roads, which will plainly be more closely grouped in the central area, are divided into *links* bounded by *nodes*. Nodes should be provided at all important intersections included in the network of traffic-significant roads. They should also be provided where the character of a length of road changes significantly — such as where a single-carriageway road becomes dual-carriageway, or a speed limit is imposed — even if there is no significant road junction at these points. Nodes throughout the road network are numbered and the network links are identified by the nodes at each end — often referred to as the A node and the B node.

The public transport network is not the same as the road network — road junctions are of less importance than stopping points and route interchanges. This is because vehicles can move about the coded road network subject only to available coded junctions, but pedestrians can only join, leave or change direction in the public transport network at stopping and interchange points. Equally, the buses themselves always remain on their predetermined routes.

In both road and public transport networks though, almost irrespective of how fine the network may be, there is a need to load trips from any one zone onto the network. Clearly each household in a zone will generate trips, all of which have to join the already-defined traffic-significant or public transport network, and although some zones are relatively small, these network-joining trip-parts cannot be handled separately. It is customary therefore for all trips generated within a zone to be assumed to emanate from a *zone centroid*, which is linked by a *centroid connector* to a node or nodes in the relevant network. The travel characteristics of the centroid connector will represent the zonal average of trips starting and finishing therein. Similarly, all trips attracted to a zone are assumed to terminate at the zone centroid via the centroid connector.

Data Requirements

The zoning system and the networks being defined, the surveys can now be undertaken. Before discussing the surveys in detail though, let us consider the objective of the surveys. This is to enable the building of a group of models (formulae) which will represent present-day travel patterns within the study area and can thereafter be used to predict future travel patterns. In the past it was not uncommon to model all trips on a combined 24-hour basis, but it is now realized that this leads to difficulties and over-simplification.

It is now more usual to model travel patterns by trip purpose — acknowledging that, for instance, the journey to work pattern is not likely to be the same as for shopping trips. Trip purposes* for which separate models are developed include:

a) between home and work-place — home-based work trips   (HBW)
b) between home and shopping area
c) between home and personal business
   (to dentist, bank, etc,)   sometimes linked
d) between home and educational   together as other-   (OHB)
   establishment   home-based trips
e) between home and social and/or
   recreational activity
f) non-home-based trips — including trips on employers'
   business from work   (NHB)

The purposes identified above as HBW, OHB and NHB are now the minimum normally acceptable in an urban transportation study.

Just as it is important to differentiate between private car trip purposes, it is also essential to model public transport trips and those of

---

* 1964 National Travel Data, and also that in respect of London car-owners, indicated that the percentage of 24-hour trips for the more important purposes was of the order of:

home to work   40%
home to shopping and personal business   20%
rest of home-based trips   35%   } 55% (OHB)
non-home-based   5%

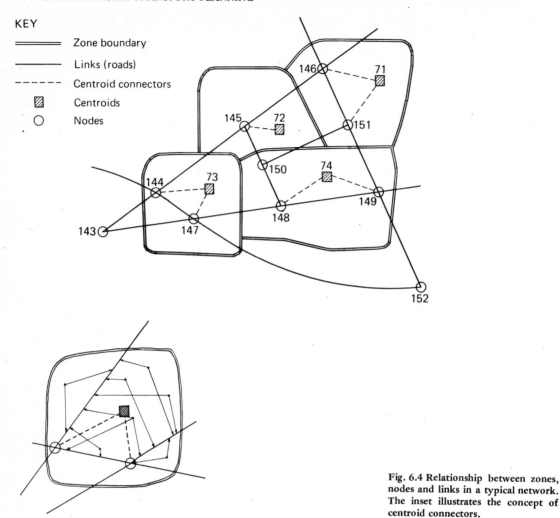

KEY

═════ Zone boundary

───── Links (roads)

- - - - - Centroid connectors

▨ Centroids

○ Nodes

Fig. 6.4 Relationship between zones, nodes and links in a typical network. The inset illustrates the concept of centroid connectors.

commercial vehicles separately from private cars and from each other. In connection with the modal choice of travellers it is also customary to differentiate between car-available and non-car-available people, using the non-car-available classification as a proxy for captive public-transport users.

The use of twenty-four-hour modelling is also becoming less common, particularly in respect of HBW trips which are largely concentrated within the morning and evening peak periods — which are themselves of crucial importance in urban transportation planning. An acceptable compromise between the desirable advantages of complete peak and off-peak modelling of all trip purposes and the extra cost of doubling the number of models, is to model HBW trips for the peak period and all other trips for either the whole 24-hour period or for a typical off-peak hour only.

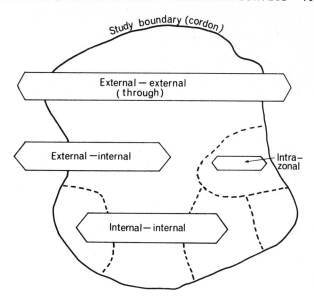

Fig. 6.5 Diagrammatic representation of the basic travel movements

Finally, travel patterns are needed in respect of four basic movements:

1) between one internal zone and another (internal-internal)
2) between an external zone, i.e. outside study area, and an internal zone (external-internal)
3) between two external zones, i.e. through the study area (external -external)
4) within an individual internal zone (intra-zonal)

The different methods of handling these different categories of movement will be dealt with in the chapter on the modelling process — at this stage it is sufficient to appreciate that separate models will need to be built for inter-zonal trips and for external trips.

There is therefore a need to collect information to enable models of varying complexity to be built in respect of:

3 purposes — HBW, OHB and NHB
2 modes — private car and public transport
2 time periods — peak and off-peak or 24-hour
2 movements — inter-zonal trips and external trips
commercial vehicles

This list is an indication of the complexity of the urban transportation study process — which will hopefully be simplified in this and the next chapter. Clearly though, the whole process is not just the sum of the models listed above — to some extent, it comprises the permutations and combinations of the list.

Surveys

The basic surveys, which are common to most urban transportation studies, and from which travel and other characteristics are derived, are:

HI	Household interview (home interview)survey	(a)(b)
RI	Roadside interview survey (and associated counts)	(a)
	Employment survey	(b)

CV	Commercial vehicle survey	(a)
PT	Public transport surveys	(a)
	Road and public transport *inventory* surveys	(a)
	Parking surveys	(b)

(a) surveys collecting data relating chiefly to movement characteristics
(b) surveys collecting data relating chiefly to zonal use characteristics

As well as the actual fieldwork of data collection as summarized above, there is also considerable desk-work to be undertaken to ascertain the zonal population and land-use statistics for the whole study area at base year. Included in that work are the classification of all employment operations within the study area in terms of the Standard Industrial Classifications and, with the aid of the Registrar-General's (National) Census of Population data, the derivation of zonal average income levels etc.

Household Interview Sample Size

The US Bureau of Public Roads' (1956) recommended HI sample sizes are, with minimum sample sizes alongside:

Population	Recommended sample percentage households	Minimum sample percentage households
under 50 000	20	10
50 − 150 000	12	5
150 − 300 000	10	3
300 − 500 000	7	2
500 − 1000 000	5	1½
over 1000 000	4	1

Recent British transportation studies have used the following HI sizes, with listed population and comparative percentages:

Study	Population	HI size	%* recomm-endation	BPR
Sheffield/Rotherham†	730 000	8000	4	5/1½
Hull	345 000	1300	1½	7/2
Gt. Yarmouth/Lowestoft	127 000	1500	5	12/5
Doncaster	387 000	2000	2	7/2
Leicester	450 000	3000	2½	7/2

* Percentage based on assumption of between 3½ and 4 persons per average household
† Household regression analysis, not category analysis.

Household Interview Survey (HI Survey)

The HI survey is designed to collect statistical data on travel habits and also on household structures and characteristics. It is perhaps the most important of all the surveys. In early transportation studies, using regression techniques of trip generation, it was customary to undertake HI surveys on a fairly large sample of the study area households. With the more frequent use of the *category analysis* method of trip generation however (Chapter 7), it is now not uncommon to rely on a smaller sample, sometimes as little as 1000 successful interviews in towns of up to about 100 000 population, basically to calibrate the standard trip rate data bank. More recently still though, other trip generation techniques have been adopted, using household regression techniques, based on more than the category analysis 1000 interviews, but still less than the early studies.

It is usual for the HI sample to be selected by taking every nth household from the electoral register or the local authority rating lists for the study area – taking care to eliminate or ignore all 'non-dwellings' from the rating lists when sampling, and to ensure that *all* local authority lists within the study area are sampled similarly. Recently, because of the noticeable trend towards 2-car households, part (perhaps 20 per cent) of the HI survey has sometimes been used to sample only within a 'higher-income bracket' households frame. This cluster sampling enables data to be collected on the most rapidly expanding sector of the community – which will be of increased importance in the future design-year work.

The HI itself is intended to ascertain the details of the household structure (number, age, and sex of occupants), occupation and employment status of household occupants, car availability, gross household income (by groups) and all journeys, irrespective of mode, made on a specified day by all members (over 5 years of age) of that household. (The use of a specified day is most appropriate in smaller towns where daily travel patterns can vary through the week. In larger towns, the specifying of one single day for all HI returns is less necessary.) The household data is particularly used to calibrate the trip rates already available from the large category analysis data banks. For each individual journey the following details would perhaps be recorded:

person making journey
origin of journey (address and land use or activity, for coding by zone)
destination of journey (as for origin)
start and finish times of journey
journey purpose (HBW etc. plus a dummy for change travel mode)
mode of travel
persons in car (if car trip)
bus route
ticket type – single, season, etc.   } only if bus trip
ticket cost for journey

and possibly, details of car park usage.

The actual interview can be conducted either by prior delivery of an explanatory letter and survey form with later collection and on-the-spot checking, or by prior delivery of explanatory letter only and personal interview of the household immediately after the survey day, the interviewer completing the form. The latter method is definitely preferable, and perhaps essential with the current smaller household sample sizes, but requires something like one hour per household interview time – largely after working hours. The first method, just checking household completion of the form can be undertaken at about two to three per hour throughout much of the day.

Roadside Interview Survey (RI Survey)

We have already looked at the need for care in defining the boundary of the study area and mentioned that this boundary would form a *cordon* around the study area. All movements *across* this cordon are inevitably external trips of one form or another — external-external or external-internal trips. These movements are not modelled in the same way as internal-internal trips, but their volume needs to be known to enable future such movements to be predicted.

As important as the cordon, if not more so, is the need for a screen line or lines across the study area, at which cross-study-area, internal-internal trips can be observed. This screen line, which should be located along zone boundaries, avoiding inlets and peninsulas and suitably sited for roadside surveys, should wherever possible follow a natural study-area dividing line — a railway route, a motorway or a river — with as few crossing points as possible. Ideally, a screen line should be unavoidably crossed by as many movements as possible, in as few locations as possible.

The purpose of the screen-line survey is to obtain origin and destination information on internal movements across the study area, which is in turn used as a check on the trips determined by the household interview survey. Because it is not possible to intercept and interview every traveller across a cordon or internal screen line, a count is also made of all vehicles and public transport passengers (see below) crossing the lines. From this count, the numbers of interviewed travellers and their inter-zonal movements can be factored-up to equate to the whole cross-line movement.

In some instances, with stations which are frequently in the busiest part of an urban area, screen-line interviewing is not carried out — the surveys being restricted solely to volumetric counts as an eventual check on household-interview-derived trip matrices. Cordon interviewing however is essential.

It is usual for roadside interviewing to be carried out on as few as possible, preferably successive, days for 12 to 16 daylight hours on all roads which cross the cordon and screen line and carry significant volumes of traffic. The usual aim is to intercept — if not interview — at least 95 per cent of all one-way traffic crossing the lines. The actual sample percentage of screen-line and cordon crossing traffic will depend on the fluctuating traffic flow through the day and can vary from 10 per cent on busy roads to 100 per cent in off-peak conditions on a minor road.

In order accurately to gross up the interview data, manual counts should be taken, by vehicle type and by traffic fluctuation period, e.g. perhaps every quarter- or half-hour in the peak period and every hour in the slack off-peak period. To gross up the daylight-hours survey data to a full and reliably average day it is also necessary to utilize automatic traffic counters over a period of several days.

The roadside interview itself consists partly of observation by the interviewer and partly of questioning the driver of the vehicle. As a vehicle approaches an interview station it is invited to stop. At the same time, as it approaches, the interviewer notes the vehicle type and number of occupants. When stationary, the purpose of the survey is briefly explained to the driver and he is asked to state his:

a) Origin address. The name of the town alone may suffice for an external trip but the actual address is needed in respect of internal trips across a screenline.
b) Destination address. If within the study area, the actual address, if not, the name of the town may suffice — subject to the zone pattern adopted; the criterion is identification of the zone.
c) Trip purpose, as specified earlier.

It has been ascertained that an interviewer can handle approximately 80 vehicles per hour in such a survey. In some locations, most commonly at central-area screen-line stations or narrow-bridge sites on town approaches, it may not be practicable to delay traffic for an actual interview. In these circumstances, a reply-paid postcard can be handed to the driver for completion at his leisure and — hopefully — return to the study team. As with all postcard response surveys there is likely to be a poor response, resulting in indeterminately biased results. This method is therefore not recommended unless absolutely unavoidable, and when adopted, the results should be used with caution.

Employment Survey

The objectives of the employment survey are two-fold — as a check on local-authority records of employment opportunities, to which trips are attracted, in the area, by zone, and to establish the population from which the sample is taken for the commercial-vehicle survey. From local-authority records and government employment statistics, supplemented by on-the-spot surveys based on rating valuation lists, it is possible to determine the total number of employment opportunities in each zone by Standard Industrial Classification (SIC) Categories.

The field survey (often in fact a postal questionnaire backed up by telephone chasing) — as opposed to the desk exercise of extracting data from local records — would also record the floor area of factories etc. in the same categories together with the number of commercial vehicles operating from each commercial address. Hence the basic questionnaire used for the employment survey would ask all centres of employment to give details of:

a) type of activity undertaken, by SIC,
b) floor area — usually covered floor space but occasionally total site area,
c) number of employees — differentiating between male and female workers,
d) number of light and heavy commercial vehicles operating from address.

Commercial Vehicle Survey (CV Survey)

Having surveyed and/or otherwise obtained details of all employment locations within the study area and the commercial vehicles operating therefrom, it is possible to select a sample of commercial vehicles for detailed study. This sample of individual vehicles would be so stratified as to provide data relating to differing sizes of firm and/or vehicle fleet. The size of the sample would vary with the size of the town but should seldom be less than 30 per cent of all commercial vehicles.

The selected sample drivers, with the agreement of the fleet operators, would be asked to log each trip they made on a specified day, recording:

a) vehicle type — plus identification details, firm's name and address, vehicle registration, etc.,

b) journey number — defining a journey as from essential stop to essential stop,

c) origin address — home garage for trip 1, first essential stop for trip 2,

d) destination address — essential stop,

e) start and finish time of trip,

f) trip purpose — firm's business or to and from home.

It is customary for an interviewer to call at the vehicle depot the day after the survey to assist the driver in completing the survey question-naire form — and to ensure its completion and collection.

Public Transport Surveys (PT Surveys)

So far we have only mentioned surveys which collect data on trips by private transport, by commercial vehicles and by the public transport vehicles themselves. We also need to collect information on public transport passengers. In metropolitan and conurbation type areas this may involve both rail and bus transport, but in other urban areas, only bus services are of major concern. The same basic techniques and requirements are generally applicable to both forms of public transport; bus services only are described below, as of greater relevance.

The prime public transport survey objective, as in other surveys, is to obtain information on the origins and destinations of travellers and on the volumes of passenger-traffic. At both cordon and screen-line roadside stations a manual volumetric count is made of all passengers crossing the lines. Observers rapidly become adept at counting passengers on passing buses — either by counting the few empty seats, or the standees, in peak periods on known-capacity buses, or by counting the few passengers on lightly used buses.

The origin and destination information is less readily obtained. Usually, observers board buses at a stop on one side of the cordon or screen line and leave the bus at the next stop, or at the central bus station. In that short space of time very little if any interviewing is possible on other than lightly loaded, off-peak services. It is customary therefore to distribute reply-paid post-card questionnaires — in the knowledge that biased, low returns are almost inevitable. To overcome passenger response reluctance as much as possible, the questionnaires are kept as simple and short as practicable and lottery-type prizes are offered for the lucky-numbered reply. As in other surveys the informa-tion required is:

   address of journey origin — not the bus stop
   address of journey destination — not the bus stop
   purpose of journey
together with:
   mode of travel prior to boarding bus (walk/other bus/train/etc.)
   mode of travel after alighting from bus.

Inventory Surveys

Having considered the collection of data on travel demands and volumes of person- and vehicle-traffic, it is necessary now to look at the collection of data relating to the facilities available for that travel. Inventories must be taken of the roads and of the bus services — link by link. We have already seen that the road network is, for the purpose of the study, divided up into homogeneous links bounded by major junctions. Information is needed on link lengths and effective widths, link capacities and associated link speeds, link accident rates and the general character of the surrounding urban fabric. Much of this information can be obtained by a desk study but details on the remainder — speeds etc. — will be collected by a standard moving-observer survey.

Like the road inventory, much of the public-transport inventory can be undertaken as a desk exercise, but it is less straightforward, being tied to individual services with fixed patterns, stops etc. The information which is needed, for each link in respect of each service using it, is the number of services per hour, the link speed (between nodes), the fare levied and the available interchange points with other services. In theory, all of this information is obtainable from timetables etc., but in practice, because bus services are frequently delayed by congestion, it is desirable to undertake field checks on speeds and delays.

The bus speed and delay survey should record overall times from stop to stop, together with boarding and alighting times and numbers at each scheduled stop. Between scheduled stops, note should be taken of reasons for, and period of, delays, e.g., due to parked and/or double-parked vehicles, right-turning vehicles causing obstruction, pedestrian crossings, general congestion etc. This survey, in addition to its use in 'building' the public transport network and models, will also be of use in determining measures appropriate to the Immediate Action Programme — rephasing traffic signals, banning right turns, restricting parking etc.

It is also useful to undertake a bus-queue survey — recording the numbers of passengers waiting at bus stops, by perhaps 2-minute intervals, arrival times of buses and numbers of passengers boarding and alighting. From this survey the actual average waiting time can be ascertained — for comparison with the operating company's idealized concept of waiting time. The adequacy of the service in meeting the demand can also thereby be assessed.

For both the road and public-transport inventories there is a common need for ascertaining times/cost from zone centroids to appropriate network nodes. These will, of course, be based on in-vehicle time for drivers, and on walk-and-wait times for the public-transport network.

Parking Surveys

The last of the surveys common to nearly all urban transportation studies are those of parking facilities and use. These (linked) surveys are important to the study process because of the influence that parking-space availability can have on actual travel demand. Basically the surveys comprise:

a) A parking space inventory — including all public- or privately-owned publicly available and private parking spaces, both on- and off-street, and the charges levied for those spaces.

b) A parking duration survey — recording all legally and illegally parked cars and the duration of their parking, by ½-hourly beat patrols noting registration numbers and matching up later.

c) A parking purpose survey — recording origin addresses, destination addresses after parking, parking purpose (work, shopping etc.), and vehicle type. The survey is undertaken by direct personal interview linked to the duration-survey ½-hour cycle.

Census Data

As well as the detailed local information collected in the course of the surveys just described, there is another valuable source of data available to the transportation planner in the Registrar-General's National Census of Population. The National Census is undertaken at ten-year intervals, on the cycle 1961, 1971, 1981 ... with an additional ten per cent sample census in 1966, which it is assumed, will be repeated in 1976, 1986 ... . Data is collected in respect of household make-up by sex, marital status and age groups, and of occupation and work-place. Commencing with the 1966 10 per cent census, data was also collected in respect of car ownership and the journey to work.

All of this data is aggregated in order to preserve confidentiality, and it is only made available by enumeration districts — hence the need to design-study area zones to be compatible with these EDs as far as possible. The census data is partly of use as a check on the household interview survey, but more particularly as the basis of the category analysis process, providing zonal population, employed population, numbers of households, cars etc, to which, after they have been checked against the HI, the standard trip rates are applied.

We have only considered the surveys and data collection specifically related to the transport side of transportation planning. There is a large amount of work involved in preparing land-use data — shopping spaces, education places, etc, — for the present-day study area and predicting this same information into the future. This work, however, is usually part of the normal routine of planning offices rather than peculiar to transportation planning, and as such, requires no further explanation in this context.

SUMMARY

a) The limits of an urban study area should be so defined to form an external cordon. Future development areas should be included in the study area which should otherwise be kept reasonably small around the urban development.

b) The study area is divided into internal zones, small enough to provide adequate travel data. Beyond the study area the whole country is divided into external zones, increasing in size with remoteness.

c) All traffic-significant roads within the study area are divided into links, bounded by nodes at important junctions. The public transport network is defined in a similar manner. Trips from each zone are linked to the network by centroid connectors.

d) Data is collected in respect of land use and travel characteristics sufficient for modelling for several purposes, for peak and off-peak periods, for movements within the study area and movements starting or finishing outside, and for movements by both private and public transport.

e) Basic surveys include:

Household interview — of a small sample, sometimes even as low as 1000 houses.

Roadside interview and counts — at cordons and screen lines.

Commercial vehicle survey — of a sample selected from a population determined by an employment survey plus other sources.

Public transport surveys — comparable to the car-driver's roadside interview.

Inventory surveys — to collect data on the characteristics of each link in both road and public transport networks.

Parking surveys — of spaces available, the use made of them, and the purpose.

f) The National Census of Population provides useful information, additional to the basic surveys, which can be used directly in the category analysis process to derive generated trips from trip rates which have been calibrated by the household interview.

7

Urban Transportation Studies – The Modelling Process

As already explained, the transportation study process consists of the development of formulae, or models, enabling future travel demands to be forecast, and alternative strategies for handling this demand to be assessed. It is not just one model, but a series of interlinked and inter-related models of varying levels of complexity, dealing with different aspects of the travel demand.

Inaccurate formulae are, of course, of limited use. The transportation study process as a whole is therefore checked and *calibrated* before it is used for future travel predictions. This is done by developing the formulae to synthesize present-day movement patterns and adjusting them until they represent observed conditions. Only when the formulae have been adjusted, or calibrated, so that they can adequately predict the present-day travel movements, are they used in true predictive mode to determine future conditions.

As we have mentioned in the previous chapter, separate models are developed for peak and off-peak trips, for trips by different purposes, for commercial vehicle trips, for trips emanating outside the study area and for trips by alternative person types (basically car-available, or not). Central to the whole process, and representing a significant proportion of all trips is the HBW peak-period trips model, and it is around that model that we shall centre the following description. It must be remembered throughout that there are many variations on the general transportation study process, and methods are continually being improved upon. The method described below is therefore just one way among several. All the methods are basically similar however and if one is understood, others will present little difficulty.

The Transportation Study Process

The basic functions included in the transportation study process are:
a) Trip-end prediction, or trip generation – the determination of the number of person trips leaving a zone, irrespective of destination, and the number of trips attracted to a zone, irrespective or origin.
b) Trip distribution – the linking of the trip origins with their destinations – or of generations and attractions.
c) Modal split – the separation of trips by private car and those by public transport.
d) Assignment – the allocation of vehicle trips between A and B to the most likely route(s) on the road network.
e) Assessment – the reason for the whole study process – is dealt with in a later chapter.

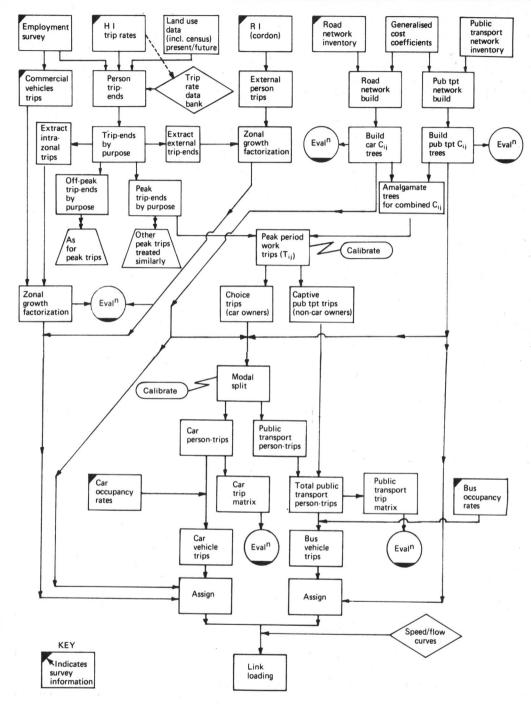

Fig. 7.1 The logic of the transportation study process

A trip — or a journey — is defined as a one-way movement by a person, normally restricted to those over the age of five, from one place to another, during all or part of which some mechanically propelled form of transport is used, i.e. wholly walk or wholly cycle trips are not usually considered.

The process as summarized above is fundamental to most forms of transport investigation, not just to the conventional transportation study of today. What makes the transportation study of today so far in advance of earlier methods is its use of the gravity model for trip distribution and the use of generalized cost as the deterrence function, or measure of spatial separation, in the gravity model.

The growth-factor distribution techniques used before adoption of the gravity model were, by their nature, incapable of representing the redistributive effect of new transport facilities — new roads or new public transport services. The gravity model can — by varying the deterrence function element. Early gravity models were based on deterrence functions of either distance or time. Generalized cost, which is effectively a combination of both these measures of spatial separation, plus the inconvenience and the actual monetary cost of a trip, permits a more realistic and basically post-distribution modelling of the modal choice of trip makers, i.e., whether the trip will be made by a car or by public transport.

The simple growth-factor techniques referred to above are still used however, both in certain parts of the transportation study modelling process (external trips and goods vehicle trips), and also in smaller towns or for inter-urban trips where redistribution is unlikely to be significant. These uses and techniques will be explained later.

Trip Generation

The first of the models in the conventional study process is that which predicts the number of trips starting and finishing in each zone. It has been found — somewhat understandably — that households with a car available to them make more — at least non-work — trips than those without. A similarly momentous discovery is that large all-adult households make more work trips than smaller ones with schoolchildren! In early studies, as mentioned in the previous chapter, it was customary to undertake large HI surveys, and from these develop study-specific formulae for zonal trip generation, by the use of multiple regression analysis techniques.

A typical regression analysis trip generation formula might be:

$$G = a_1 x_1 + a_2 x_2 + a_3 x_3 \ldots + K$$

Where G = number of trips per zone for a specified purpose,
a_1, a_2, etc. = coefficients determined by the regression process,
x_1, x_2, etc. = zonal planning input factors (independent variables)
K = a constant

Typical zonal planning input factors might include employed population, car ownership per head, household rateable value (as a proxy for household income), and residential density. The formulae are usually developed by standard computer programs and should always be built up rather than down, i.e. only adding a further independent variable if it can be shown to improve the fit of the overall formula. The validity of the regression formula developed in this way is checked by measurement of the correlation coefficient R, which should approach its maximum value of 1 as closely as possible; values exceeding 0.9 are common.

Although zonal regression analysis has now been almost entirely superseded by the category analysis technique in respect of trip generations, it remains a frequently used method for the determination of trip attractions. The attraction formula may be developed as a function of such zonal variables as total employment, floor area, differential SIC employment, etc.

Category analysis, which was developed and published in Britain in 1967, by Wootton and Pick, is based on the use of trip rates by household category rather than by zone – the results being aggregated later to give zonal trips. When trip generation is considered at household level, Wootton and Pick assumed that trip rates will remain constant in the future, and that a trip rate can be established for each household, categorized by only three factors – car ownership, household structure, and household income. Wootton and Pick's original category analysis technique used six levels of household income, six sets of household structure characteristics, and three levels (0, 1, 2+) of car ownerships, making a total of 108 categories for each of six purposes and three modes. Recently however these early category analysis programs have been expanded to 180 categories, by adopting a wider range of household income groups.

Basically, data banks are built up of household trip rates, by categories, car availability and purpose, derived from household interviews in earlier, large household surveys. These surveys will have been of sufficient size to permit of adequate statistics in each cell of the category and purpose matrix cubes. When a small HI survey is made, preparatory to applying category analysis, the trip-rate data resulting from this survey is used initially to adjust the data banks, being later absorbed therein, for use in the next study. Then, using census data, the number of households of each category in each zone is determined, and the appropriate trip rate applied thereto. Thus, there might be 50 households in a zone, each with gross income in the range £2000 to £2500, owning one car (and therefore a car-available household) and with one employed and one non-employed resident adult; each household making an average of 0.88 HBW trips per 24-hour day, and thereby giving a total zonal trip generation of 44 trips *from those households*.

Since the initial development of the category analysis technique, other packages have been developed, using the same principles. Most of these more recent packages use a smaller number of categories. For a perhaps extreme example, in the somewhat 'broad brush' *Strategic Plan for the South East* (of England), R. Travers Morgan & Partners developed 24-hour trip rates by 9 categories only – 0,1,2+ cars and 0,1,2+ resident workers. These trip rates were calculated for three basic trip purposes and in relation to car-available and no-car-available households, i.e. 6 category matrix squares rather than cubes.

No matter whether the generated trips are the result of analysis

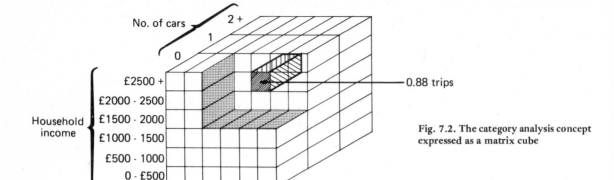

Fig. 7.2. The category analysis concept expressed as a matrix cube

by 108, 180, or even 9 categories, and whether or not the attracted trips are derived by regression analysis or by a form of category analysis, clearly the total internal trips generated should balance the attracted trips. It would be highly unlikely for this balance to be achieved automatically or by chance — so there is a need to balance the totals. The calculation of trip generations is likely to be more accurate than that of trip attractions, so it is usual for all trip attractions to be scaled up by a common factor to equate to the total generations.

Trip Distribution

Having therefore ascertained the total number of trips by all modes which start from each zone for a specific purpose and similarly the corrected number of trips which arrive in each zone, the next task is to link them up. Effectively, at this moment, we have a matrix of empty cells, but with column and row totals known, or:

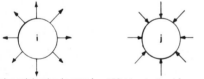

200 trips originating in zone i   150 trips destined for zone j

What we *need* to know is how many of the trips starting in zone i will end in zone j — and how many in each other zone i.e.:

The basic principle which is applied in internal trip distribution is that trips will be made to a given zone in direct proportion to its relative attractiveness and in some form of decreasing proportion to the separation of the attracting zone from the originating zone. In its simplest form this principle is expressed as

$$T_{ij} \propto \frac{G_i A_j}{d^n}$$

where T_{ij} = trips from zone i to zone j
        G_i = total number of trips generated in zone i
        A_j = total number of trips attracted to zone j
        d   = distance or other measure of spatial separation
        n   = a constant (usually assumed to be between 1 and 2·5)
which, for its obvious similarity to Newton's 1686 concept of gravitational attraction is known as a Gravity Model. The relationship is more
usually expressed however, for any given trip purpose, as

$$T_{ij} = KG_i A_j F(C_{ij})$$

where T_{ij}, G_i, A_j are as before, and
        $F(C_{ij})$ is some function of the separation of the zones i and j,
        a deterrence function
and   K is a constant.
Once F and K are determined, clearly all of the known zonal Gs, As and
C_{ij}s can be input to complete a matrix of inter-zonal trips T_{ij}.

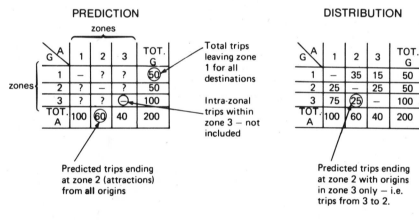

Fig. 7.3 Two matrices —
results of trip prediction
and trip distribution

Generalized Cost

In recent years, the favoured, and most commonly used, measure of
deterrence is the perceived interzonal *generalized cost* — that is, what
the traveller, albeit perhaps unconsciously, *thinks* it costs him to travel
from A to B. For each pair of zones therefore, the total cost of a car
trip, and also of a largely public transport trip, are determined. In the
case of a car trip this would comprise:
a) driving time cost,
b) car operating costs as perceived by the driver, i.e. distance costs,
c) parking charge,
d) cost of extra time spent waiting or walking from car park to actual
    destination (and from home to home car park where applicable)
For any given interzonal trip the cost between each of the two zone
centroids and the appropriate actual network nodes is added to the
least-cost journey through the whole network between the zones. For

The Gravity Distribution Model

The general description of the gravity distribution model is, as quoted in the main text:

$$T_{ij} = KG_iA_jF(C_{ij})$$

where $F(C_{ij})$ is the deterrence, or trip decay, function and is based on the *generalized cost* of the journey from i to j.

The trip decay function is usually in one of three basic decreasing forms:

a) a power function: $\qquad\qquad\qquad\qquad F(C_{ij}) = C_{ij}^{-n}$

b) an exponential function: $\qquad\qquad\quad F(C_{ij}) = e^{-\beta C_{ij}}$

c) a gamma function, attributed to J.C. Tanner: $F(C_{ij}) = e^{-\beta C_{ij}} C_{ij}^{-n}$

where n is a power, usually less than 2, and when used alone usually between 1 and 2, and β is a constant, usually less than 0.2 and often less than 0.1.

It has been found that the power function, which was widely used in early, particularly American, studies is more appropriate to longer-distance, basically inter-urban (in Europe) trips. The exponential function has been used in many recent British studies and has been found to be particularly appropriate in shorter-distance, intra-urban trips. The Tanner function offers the opportunity to combine the advantages of each of the other functions.

The constant K in the general formula is effectively two balancing constants combined together — one each for correcting the numbers of generations, and attractions. Thus

$$K = a_ib_j$$

where $\qquad\qquad\qquad a_i\Sigma_jT_{ij} = G_i$

and $\qquad\qquad\qquad\quad b_j\Sigma_iT_{ij} = A_j$

The determination of each of the constants in the distribution model is known as *calibration*, which will be dealt with later.

a trip including one or more public transport links and walk links thereto, the public transport generalized cost would be made up of:
a) cost of walking time to bus stop (by notional centroid link),
b) cost of waiting time at bus stop,
c) cost of travelling time on bus,
d) bus fare,
e) cost of bus interchange waiting time — where appropriate,
f) further c) and d) — where appropriate,
g) cost of walking time from bus stop to destination (by notional centroid link).

The least-cost journey from any one zone to another is determined by a process known as *building trees*. Were it not capable of being undertaken by the computer, this process, like much of the transportation study process, would be very time consuming – involving as it does the costing of the routes from each zone to every other.

Generalized Cost

Generalized cost for a specific mode can be expressed generally as:

$$C_{ij} = a_1 t_{ij} + a_2 e_{ij} + a_3 d_{ij} + p_j \, (+\delta)$$

where C_{ij} = generalized cost

t_{ij} = travel time from i to j

e_{ij} = excess time (access, waiting, etc.)

d_{ij} = distance from i to j

p_j = terminal cost at destination end of trip (j)

δ = the inherent modal handicap – a calibrating statistic sometimes irreverently referred to as a 'fudge' factor, representing such immeasurable factors as comfort and convenience

a_1, a_2, a_3 = constants representing the values of the components, a_1 being the average value of travelling time. a_2 is usually taken as $2a_1$, on the behavioural observation that excess time is, in fact, valued by travellers at twice actual travelling time.

To achieve greater stability over time, bearing in mind that the purpose of a transportation study is to investigate strategies for a (relatively) remote design year, it is suggested that the generalized cost formula be stabilized on the rising value of time, by dividing throughout by a_1, thus converting the cost from price units to time-like units. This effectively assumes that the impedance to travel, in time-like units, will remain stable over time. Thus the expression normally used is:

$$C_{ij} = t_{ij} + \frac{a_2}{a_1} e_{ij} + \frac{a_3}{a_1} d_{ij} + \frac{p_j}{a_1} \left(+ \frac{\delta}{a_1} \right)$$

Separate least-cost journey trees would be built for car trips and public transport trips, and from these trees, zone-to-zone cost matrices could be produced for each mode. But we are still working in terms of total trips generated in or attracted to a zone – irrespective of mode. In order to distribute the trips in their person-trip form therefore, the cost matrices need to be amalgamated. At this stage in the model development the two costs for each zone-to-zone movement are amalgamated, often in proportion to the split of present-day travel by each mode. From this exercise a matrix of composite generalized cost is determined – and it is this matrix of costs which is used in the distribution process.

Modal Split

The distribution made, in terms of person trips, the next step is to separate the car trips from those made by public transport. For this

Building a Least-cost Journey Tree on Node F

(Moore's Algorithm)

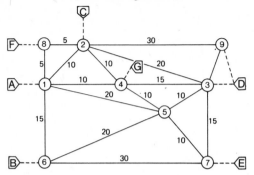

Assume all centroid links are identical in cost, at 5 units, and ignore in tree building process — therefore starting tree at node 8. Determine tree by moving forward one link at a time:

Link	Cost	Link combination	Total cost	Least cost to Node
8 - 1	5			1
8 - 2	5			2
1 - 2	10	8 - 1 - 2	15	
1 - 4	10	8 - 1 - 4	15	4
1 - 5	20	8 - 1 - 5	25	5
1 - 6	15	8 - 1 - 6	20	6
2 - 4	10	8 - 2 - 4	15	
2 - 3	20	8 - 2 - 3	25	3
2 - 9	30	8 - 2 - 9	35	9 (But to D via 3.)
4 - 3	15	8 - 1 - 4 - 3	30	
4 - 5	10	8 - 1 - 4 - 5	25	
5 - 3	10	8 - 1 - 5 - 3	35	
5 - 7	10	8 - 1 - 5 - 7	35	7
6 - 5	20	8 - 1 - 6 - 5	40	
6 - 7	30	8 - 1 - 6 - 7	50	
3 - 9	10	8 - 2 - 3 - 9	35	
3 - 7	15	8 - 2 - 3 - 7	40	
9 - 3	10	8 - 2 - 9 - 3	45	

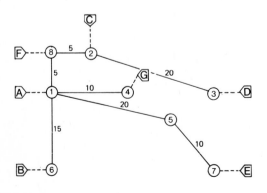

process it is customary to assume that people who do not have a car available will be captive public transport passengers. These trips would be assigned, without further consideration, to the public transport system.* People with a car available to them, however, do not necessarily always use it – they have a choice of travelling either by car or by public transport – a modal choice. This choice is assumed to be based on *their perception* of the generalized cost of each of the alternative modes of travel and this is customarily expressed in the form:

$$\frac{T_{ij}{}^{car}}{T_{ij}{}^{all\ modes}} = \frac{F(C_{ij}{}^{car})}{F(C_{ij}{}^{all\ modes})}$$

Hence, when costs by each mode are the same then the modal split will be 50/50.

Another method of modelling the modal split is by the use of diversion curves, usually determined from the survey data. The London Transportation Study developed such curves to model the percentage of trips by public transport from the ratio of time by public transport against time by private transport.

A recent development relating to the modal split aspect of modelling procedures is the amalgamation of the modal choice with the distribution process. It is not considered appropriate to expand on this development in this context – the interested reader is referred to other sources, listed in the Bibliography.

Assignment

By the application of average car and bus occupancy rates relating to trip purposes, it is then possible, from the modal split model output, to build matrices of vehicle trips. The next step must then be to load these trips onto the network/system – to *assign* them. Least-cost journey trees have already been built for all inter-zone journeys and at this stage in the modelling process it is not unrealistic to load all vehicle trips onto these least-cost routes. This is known as all-or-nothing assignment and, other than for public transport assignments, is not usually considered as realistically modelling the actual road loadings.

Other methods of assignment commonly used in the predictive application (see below) of the model are those known as capacity restraint and multi-route. Both of these techniques take account of the unlikelihood of all trips using the single least-cost route. The capacity restraint method specifically takes account of the fact that as traffic is incrementally loaded onto a link, it becomes increasingly less attractive to travellers. This loading causes other nearby links to assume the role of least cost alternative, thereby amending the journey cost tree for the next increment of load.

The multi-route method of assignment is based on the concept that the driver of a vehicle does not in fact know which is the least-cost journey route, but only the route which he *thinks* is the least costly. The method therefore depends on the repeated random selection of each link cost from a number of possible costs distributed over, say, ± 20 per cent around a mean of the actual, measured link cost. The least-cost journey tree from any one zone is built up from one series of these randomly selected link costs and is used to assign, on an

*In some variations of the transportation study process, this split into 'captive-public-transport' and 'choice' travellers is made before the distribution process. Captive public transport trips would be distributed using only the public transport C_{ij} matrix, while only the choice trips would be distributed using the combined C_{ij} matrix. The choice trips would then, after distribution, be modally split as above.

Capacity Restraint Assignment

The capacity restraint assignment technique depends on the relationship between the volume of traffic using a link and the speed at which
that traffic can move – the speed/flow relationship. In general, the
speed/flow relationship of a road link is of the form:

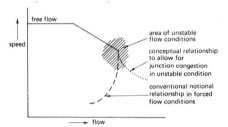

If, say, 50 per cent of an i-j travel demand is assigned to a least-cost
route this will, if it exceeds the free flow limit of any link, cause the
average speed to drop, in turn increasing the travel cost on that link.
If the least-cost journey tree is now re-assessed, it may be that a different
route will be determined, omitting that link. If now a further, say 30
per cent of the i to j travel demand is assigned to the new route, this
may in turn cause the flow on another link to exceed the free-flow
limit. The resulting link travel cost increase may so change the tree that
the original route is once again the least-cost one, and a further portion
of the demand is assigned to that route. And so on.

all-or-nothing basis, all of the trips originating from that zone. Separate
least-cost journey trees are built for each originating zone, based in each
case on different series of randomly selected link costs. This causes
different batches of trips on roughly similar journeys to be assigned
over different links. *See* example.

Calibration

So far, all of the steps and processes described have been those which
are initially applied to the base year – the year of the surveys – and as
mentioned earlier, only the HBW peak period internal trips model has
so far been considered. The base year conditions, which are clearly
already known, are modelled for precisely that reason – in order to
compare the modelled, or synthesized, results with the observed, or
actual, conditions. This enables the model to be *calibrated* – tuned or
adjusted so that it accurately (or reasonably accurately) represents the
present conditions. Wherever possible throughout the process, the
predicted results are compared with actual observations, and factoring
constants are inserted to equate results.

Perhaps the most important of the calibration exercises is the
calibration of the distribution model – the determination of the K and
the F in the formula mentioned above. The deterrence function F is

Simplified Example of Multi-route Assignment

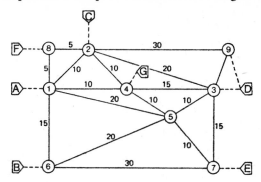

Mean costs for each link are as shown on diagram above. Consider only 3 random costs per link, ± 20%. Then:

Link	Cost	Cost	Cost	Link	Cost	Cost	Cost	Link	Cost	Cost	Cost
1-2	8	10	12	2-4	8	10	12	5-6	16	20	24
1-4	8	10	12	2-8	4	5	6	5-7	8	10	12
1-5	16	20	24	2-9	24	30	36	6-7	24	30	36
1-6	12	15	18	4-3	12	15	18	7-3	12	15	18
1-8	4	5	6	4-5	8	10	12	9-3	8	10	12
2-3	16	20	24	5-3	8	10	12				

Journey cost A-D, choosing costs at random from 3 possible costs above, is cheapest of:

1 - 2 - 3	1 - 4 - 3	1 - 5 - 3
8 + 24 = 32	12 + 15 = 27	16 + 8 = 24
		Least-cost route A-D

Journey cost F-D, choosing costs at random *again* from above, is best of:

8 - 2 - 3	8 - 2 - 4 - 3	8 - 1 - 4 - 3	8 - 1 - 5 - 3
6 + 24 = 30	6 + 10 + 12 = 28	5 + 8 + 12 = 25	5 + 16 + 12 = 33
		Least-cost route F-D	

Journey cost A-E, using the A-tree costs already chosen, above, is best of:

1 - 4 - 5 - 7	1 - 5 - 7	1 - 6 - 7
12 + 12 + 10 = 34	16 + 10 = 26	15 + 24 = 39
	Least-cost route A-E	

Journey cost F-E, using the F-tree costs already chosen, above, is best of:

8 - 1 - 4 - 5 - 7	8 - 2 - 4 - 5 - 7	8 - 1 - 5 - 7
5 + 8 + 10 + 8 = 31	6 + 10 + 10 + 8 = 34	5 + 18 + 8 = 29
		Least-cost route F-E

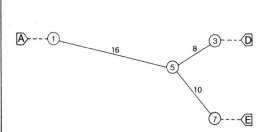

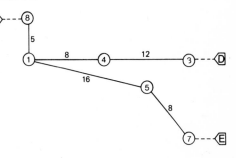

determined by comparison of observed and synthesized trip cost distributions. This distribution is obtained by summing, for each purpose, the total number of trips within the study area, irrespective of origin or destination, in blocks of, say, 0-2, 2-4, 4-6, etc. units of cost (time-like units). The function is adjusted until the shapes of the observed and synthesized distributions correspond adequately. The balancing constant K is determined in respect of each ij pair, by comparison of the matrix row and column totals in observed and synthesized matrices, and effectively corrects the scale of the distribution.

A further check on the quality of the calibration is made when the total (as opposed to one-purpose) base year synthesized flows are assigned to the road network. At this stage, although the synthesized flows on individual roads cannot necessarily be expected to correspond with observed flows, it is reasonable to expect a significant proportion of corridor flows, i.e. groups of more-or-less parallel roads, across a screen line or cordon to correspond within say ± 25 per cent, depending on the actual link flow level.

Other Models

So far we have only described the modelling process applicable to HBW trips in the peak period. Basically, the whole of the same process would be repeated for the other specified trip purposes and for the off-peak period – for which a representative hour is usually modelled. Because of cost considerations, however, trips other than HBW are sometimes modelled on a 24-hour basis, the results being factored, to give peak-hour flows for amalgamation with the more important (in the peak period) work trips. Similarly, the modelled peak period HBW trips would also be factored to give 24-hour flows for amalgamation with the other modelled flows. Irrespective of how they are modelled, however, by peak and off-peak hours (derived from peak and off-peak period consideration), or by 24-hour flows, the procedures would be the same as already described.

Neither commercial-vehicle trips nor external or through trips are modelled in the same way as previously described however. It is generally accepted that none of such trips are suitable for generation by category analysis or for distribution by the gravity model process – basically because the techniques are insufficiently developed for these purposes. (Although there are category analysis procedures for determining commercial-vehicle trips, these are not used as frequently or as commonly as the person-trip procedures). The customary process for modelling commercial, externals, and through trips is by building a present-day origin and destination matrix from observed data, applying zonal growth factors for future years and distributing by the Furness or similar technique. (See Chapter 10 for description and worked example of the growth factor/Furness procedures). The end results are then added to the outputs of the other models for overall assignment.

Predictive Mode

Having then built adequate and proven models for the base year conditions and movement patterns, the package of models is ready to be used in a predictive mode. The initial requirement is for zone-by-zone land use and general planning data and population characteristics for the design-year conditions. As has already been mentioned (Chapter 1) a single estimate of the most likely land use in the design year is required for evaluation purposes.

Given the best available estimate of design-year zonal population and planning characteristics, application of the category analysis program enables total internal zonal trip generations to be determined, purpose by purpose. Similarly, the regression formulae determined for the base year can be used to produce total internal zonal trip attractions. As already mentioned, zonal growth factors for goods, external, and through trips can also be determined.

From all of these exercises a set of purpose matrices with G and A (generation and attraction) totals but with empty T_{ij} cells can be produced. Clearly, because these hollow matrices are dependent solely on the single land-use input, they will be common to all alternative transportation strategies applied thereto. Only the individual T_{ij} cell figures will vary from strategy to strategy as redistribution occurs. Equally it is clear that the predictive trip generation process assumes that trip-making characteristics remain constant in terms of the categories adopted. For example, a highly paid artisan in a two-car, two-employed-resident household will make the same number of trips in 1991 as a similarly paid (in real money terms) 2-car executive and working wife in the 1970s.

Future network details of the Do-nothing and each of the alternative Do-something strategies must now, separately, be fed into the modelling process. From these details, future C_{ij} matrices and least-cost journey trees are built up in respect of each strategy – they will vary considerably. The full distribution, modal split, and assignment modelling processes, by peak or off-peak period, by purpose and by person-type, are then applied in respect of each of the future strategies. From the results of these modelling processes the alternative strategies can be evaluated on a comparative basis. The economic evaluation is based on the modally split matrices without assignment but the operational and environmental assessments require assignment to be made to future networks, and these are usually made by the capacity-restraint or multi-route methods. The initial assignment to the Do-nothing network might well however be a cheaper, all-or-nothing one, to be used basically as a desire-line indication of demand patterns*.

Briefly then, we have described the more important techniques and processes involved in the transportation study package, and in later chapters the problems of detailed option formulation and urban option evaluation will be considered. It is important however at this stage to remember that the transportation study process suffers from several inherent defects. No-one suggests that the present process is perfect – it is continually being developed and improved. It is useful therefore to recognize some of the more troublesome shortcomings of the process, in order that the results will be viewed with the appropriate scepticism.

* For evaluating purposes however, the Do-nothing network assignment should also be made by capacity restraint or multi-route methods.

As we have already hinted at, one considerable shortfall of the process is the fixed nature of the G and A totals across alternative transport strategies. Among other things this prevents the modelling of any change in trip production due to increased accessibility, i.e. there is no facility for modelling generated traffic, only redistributed traffic.

Another of the more obvious disadvantages of the system as applied at present is the distribution by *overall* trip attraction, which merely indicates so many jobs in a zone irrespective of job type. This can mean, due to residential distribution anomalies, that all the executive-type residents in one zone are modelled as attracted to a factory in a nearby zone whereas the artisans and labourers in another zone are modelled as attracted to the central business district. Because overall long-term trip patterns are considered, however, this disadvantage is not quite so disastrous as may at first appear — anomalies tend to be averaged out.

Finally of course, the whole modelling process — in the mathematical parts of which an overall accuracy of within ± 20 per cent would not be unreasonable — is dependent on future land-use predictions, which are notoriously, and acknowledged so to be, unreliable. The saving grace of the whole process is that it is one of comparison and ranking of alternatives, and not a one-off individual assessment. Each alternative is compared with each other, all of which have been built on the same, admittedly inaccurate foundation. The actual traffic flows etc. in the preferred strategy may be far from accurate but the ranking of strategies is unlikely to be significantly incorrect.

SUMMARY

a) The transportation study process comprises a number of inter-related models which enable future travel conditions to be predicted.

b) The processes — basically trip generation, trip distribution, modal split, and assignment, are applied initially to the base-year planning data in order to predict synthesized movements for comparison with observed movements. Once the models are adjusted to predict present-day conditions, they can be used in predictive mode to ascertain likely design-year travel movements.

c) A recommended trip generation process is known as category analysis, of which there are several different types. Prediction of trip attractions is usually by regression analysis.

d) Trip distribution is customarily done by use of a gravity model using generalized cost as a measure of zonal separation. For goods and external trips however, distribution is still usually done by a simple growth-factor technique.

e) After distribution, person trips are divided between cars and public transport by a modal-split process, usually again based on generalized cost. Person trips are converted to vehicle trips by application of occupancy factors.

f) Public and private vehicles are assigned to actual roads by one of three methods — All-or-nothing (always used for public transport), capacity restraint, or multi-route.

g) In predictive mode, the same techniques are applied to design-year planning data. This means a fixed set of G and A totals in the future matrices, individual cells in which will vary for each of the future year systems — the Do-nothing and the several Do-somethings.

8

The Development of Urban Transportation Options

So far we have looked at the technical processes involved in a transportation study — how to build the models and how to use them in predictive mode. We need now to look at the object of the predictive use of the models — indeed, at the objective of the study process. Clearly, as intimated earlier, this overall objective is to assist in the determination of a preferred urban-transport strategy.

But the transportation study process is only a method for predicting travel demands and, by means of evaluation techniques, which will be described in the next chapter, assessing the comparative effectiveness of alternative strategies in meeting that demand. The transportation study process itself cannot develop these strategies — it can only provide the means for comparing the strategies which are input for appraisal. The preferred strategy resulting from an urban transportation study can therefore only be as good as the conception and the inspiration applied to the development of the input alternatives. It is clear therefore that the development of the options for testing is of fundamental importance in the transportation study process.

The Do-nothing Strategy

Central to this process is the Economic Base, or so-called Do-nothing (DN) strategy. The DN strategy is the base against which each alternative is compared. It is always the initial option; it should preferably be the strategy from inspection of which the new options are developed. It represents, within certain technical limitations, the travel conditions likely to prevail in the future design year if no major future capital commitments are entered into, i.e. it is not simply present-day conditions with future travel patterns imposed thereon.

The phrase Do-nothing is itself a misnomer — nothing really stands still for fiteen years into the future. It is better conceived of as a Do-minimum strategy in respect of capital investment. For testing purposes, it is nevertheless expected to be an integrated and viable strategy. This latter requirement means that the DN strategy has to be 'built' as carefully as any of the possible, capital-intensive, new options. It is built from the same components as all options:

    the public transport service
    the private car restraint measures
    the optimum use of existing road networks
    the provision of new roads.

In the DN strategy the simplest of all components to define is the road network. Clearly all existing roads and those under construction at the time of the study will be included. Equally clearly, road schemes at an early stage in preparation will not be included. Between these two extremes there is some, albeit limited, scope for judgement as to whether or not a scheme is to be included.

The guiding principle should be to keep the number of unstarted schemes admitted to a minimum. Schemes included in the DN strategy clearly cannot be tested within the transportation study process. If too many unstarted schemes are included in the DN strategy then the implementation programme for too many years ahead will be committed — *without adequate justification*. Of equal importance: if too many schemes are included in the DN strategy, the probably available funds will be reduced by the cost of the schemes, making option development that much more restricted and difficult.

Although basically only inescapably committed 'testable' road schemes should be included in the DN strategy, there are other road schemes which are not open to testing at the county level. Into this category, at urban or county level, fall the motorways and trunk roads of the national network. These roads are customarily planned on a nationwide basis and once so determined should normally be accepted as fixed in the urban or county context, and incorporated in the DN strategy.

The restraint and public transport measures included in the DN strategy are less easily determined. The provision of parking spaces should be accounted for in the same basic manner as for road schemes — only inescapably committed public or privately owned parks should be included. Similarly, unless the urban transport authority is already engaged in implementing a published policy of reducing roadside parking places, no reduction in parking space should be permitted in the DN strategy. Inclusion of such a move, particularly before a policy decision, would lay the transport planner open to a charge of making decisions without adequate support. The determination of parking charges in the DN strategy, bearing in mind the need for viability, is less straightforward however and will depend on the level of public transport service available in the future.

Public Transport Services

On a national scale, the use of public transport has declined steadily over the last few years, with the growth in car ownership and use. Because of their traditionally commercial operating practices, and the need for a break-even financial structure, this has entailed the bus industry reducing services and raising fares — inevitably thereby aggravating the problem and accelerating the decline in patronage. Extrapolation of this trend, and, initially at any rate, maintaining the break-even requirement, indicates that the number of passengers may well drop below 50 per cent of present-day patronage within a 10 to 15-year period, and in extreme conditions to around 25 per cent.

Bearing in mind that despite the possibility of a continuing increase in car ownership there will long remain a captive public transport market — estimated at some 50 per cent of the population of Britain for some, if not all, of their desired trips — it may be acceptable for a quasi-political decision to be taken, relating to the DN strategy, to hold the decline at, say, 33 per cent of today's level. This political commitment would then be taken as a committed expenditure during the plan period, and it would presumably entail, at least initially, some measure of revenue support, because it would only be necessary or effective if the predicted break-even service level were lower than the commitment level.

Restraint Measures

We have then, in the DN strategy, a fixed road network, a fixed number of car parking spaces and now determined public transport service level. Bearing in mind that the modelling process assumes — not wholly illogically — that the overall number of trips made from each origin zone is not a variable, the level of restraint necessary to hold car trips to available space must next be determined. Unless this is done, the DN system will not in fact be workable, it will be an unrealistic alternative.

The only variables affecting the trips made from any one zone are the competitive trip destinations and the mode by which the trips are made and both of these variables are affected by any imposed car-trip restraint. If the parking charge is varied, then the spatial separation measured by the generalized cost will vary in respect of car trips only. If the variation in parking charge is sufficient, the relative attraction of the destination zone will vary and so will the chosen mode of the trip. The number of car trips can thus be constrained to the capacity of the parks and, to a lesser extent, of the road system, and the frustrated car trips will divert to the bus mode.

The capacity of the whole road system is perhaps best measured by the volume/capacity condition of selected links and junctions. If the road system cannot adequately accommodate as much movement as can be accommodated in the existing car parks and on-street spaces, it may be necessary to increase parking charges even more, to further divert car trips to the bus mode.

A major difficulty in developing any option — DN or Do-something — in almost every town, is the 'reverse gearing' due to the number of non-publicly-controllable parking spaces. Although the transport planner can test the effects of imposed parking charges on public car parks, these can only affect those trips destined for controllable parks, which are sometimes as little as only 50 per cent of the total parking spaces in the area.

Balancing the DN Strategy

Clearly the imposition of penal parking charges will create an annual profit from car parking which, for planning purposes at least, might reasonably be counted against the cost, throughout the plan period, of the revenue support to public transport. At the same time too, the diversion of trips to public transport caused by the parking charges will probably enable the bus service to approach more nearly to a break-even condition than initially predicted. The whole process of making the DN system work — and indeed, the alternative Do-something system also — is an iterative process of trial and error. However, a 'feel' for the inter-relationship of fares, parking charges etc., which must inevitably be specific to any single area, is soon obtained with practice. The experience gained in development of the workable DN system is also a great help in later developing the alternative Do-something systems.

The now workable DN system (or strategy) is the base against which each alternative strategy is compared. The minimized expenditure, including that committed in formulating the workable system, within the plan period — i.e. the new road and car park schemes actually about to start and the overall total net subsidy — has now to be deducted from the total planning expectation of funds for the plan period. The balance is the total available for the alternative Do-something strategies.

Option Development

Ideally perhaps, transport plans would be built up piece by piece with the incremental advantages or benefits of each element determined before it is added to the overall plan. But this approach is basically at odds with the concept of the essentially integrated system. It smacks of individual scheme assessment, which is not appropriate in urban areas. Another approach, slightly better, but still not wholly appropriate to the comprehensive, integrated system approach, is to hold one major component — say the road network — constant, while varying other components — public transport service, restraint etc. Better by far, the multiple 'sketch-plan' approach to option development, each plan being a whole (or major part) system, each one comprehensive within itself.

All of these methods entail many separate runs of the transportation models — at considerable cost. The scheme-by-scheme option development theoretically necessitates a full distribution exercise for each new scheme or policy. The fixed/variable component approach necessitates a geometric multiplicity of tests, involving comparing every combination against all others. The sketch-plan approach entails the progressive reduction of plans down to a manageable number of more finalized options. This could involve a large number of model runs, but by subjectively grouping sketch plans in terms of similar components this approach is probably the most sensible.

Accepting a sketch-plan approach, the development of options should be aimed at the formulation of at least three options for full, quantified testing. These three initial options should be designed to vary widely in their mix of components, and are often designated as:

car oriented

middle-of-the-road

public transport oriented.

Preferably, these initial options should be developed from inspection of the results of the future year travel patterns and the problem areas shown up by the DN strategy, but this is not always possible for timing reasons.

Strategy Concepts

Purely as an indication of the type of schemes and policies appropriate to the three wide-ranging initial strategies, these might be:

a) Car-oriented strategy: bus service at similar or little higher level than adopted in the DN strategy (including negligible or zero revenue support). Additional parking spaces in or near town centre, hopefully sufficient to meet (or at least approach) the likely demand. New road network A, designed to ease car access into town centre. Parking charges as low as possible within constraint of 'commercial break-even' and yet to reach an approximately balanced demand. Available funds will seldom permit an extreme car-oriented strategy, some measure of restraint is almost always necessary.

b) Public-transport-oriented strategy (basically bus-oriented in foreseeable future in most towns): greatly improved bus service, with increased frequencies and improved penetration. Bus regularity and reliability enhanced by major network (rather than isolated lengths) of bus lanes and bus-ways. Possibility of bus revenue support in early years until restraint measures bite. Few, if any, additional parking spaces in central area and many of the existing spaces not available before 0930. High central-area parking charges for other than short-stay parkers. New, low-charge or free car parks on urban periphery linked to peak hour park-and-ride services (if warranted by average journey lengths). New road network B, incorporating bus lanes wherever possible and generally designed to assist (perhaps) non-radial movements, leisure, educational trips, etc.

c) Middle-of-the-road strategy: as implied, less severe than either of the above two extremes — a compromise option hoping for the best of all worlds. New road network C.

To indicate the sort of split, the available funds which are usually, and preferably, held constant over at least the initial batch of options might be pre-determined or evolve at something like these proportions:

	System a Car-oriented	System b Bus-oriented	System c Middle-of-the-road
New roads	80%(network A)	45%(network B)	60%(network C)
New car parks	15%(central area)	40%(periphery)	30%(periphery)
Bus subsidy	5%	15%	10%

It is only desirable that these initial strategies be built to a common total expenditure — later options can explore different levels of expenditure if advantageous.

Within the limits of common sense, the new road schemes in network A should not be repeated in either network B or network C. This ideal is hard to achieve but at least it is not unreasonable to require that few, if any schemes should be common to all three road networks. It is customary, when 'building' the road element of the strategies to select possible schemes from a pool of pre-examined and costed schemes. This approach, while obviously sensible, should not be allowed to exercise a constraint on the choice of perhaps more comprehensively-oriented, newly conceived schemes.

Just as the DN strategy had to be made workable, so too do the Do-something strategies. Similar exercises must be undertaken to balance the parking provision with the parking charges and public transport availability, and all within the total level of funds. The 'feel' obtained when balancing the DN system will be invaluable and save time in the same iterative process for the initial options.

Optimization

But there is no intention that a choice of best-of-three made from these initial options should become the final strategy. Further optimization options are usually developed after assessment of the initial series of options and possibly also after sounding out public opinion on the initially favoured strategy. By spreading the balance, or mix, of the initial options as wide as sensibly possible and including a central option, it is hoped to ease the optimization process.

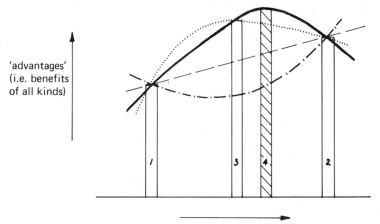

'advantages' (i.e. benefits of all kinds)

Emphasis on component
(e.g. increasing public transport orientation of option)

LOGIC AND KEY

If only options 1 and 2 are investigated, the 'advantage curve' can be any of the 4 lines shown. As soon as the 'middle of the road' option number 3 is tested, curves

—·—·— and — — —

are shown to be inappropriate, leaving, as possibilities

·············· and ———, the

latter being found to be correct in the optimization test No. 4.

Fig. 8.1 The strategy optimization concept

The actual optimization process is inevitably one fraught with difficulties. Were only, say, the public transport service being varied, with a fixed road network and level of restraint, optimization would perhaps be relatively easy. The need to economize on the number of options however necessitates the variation of all options across all components, which in turn means considerable subjectivity in the optimization. It is clearly too much to expect to be able, correctly, to hit upon the optimum strategy at first attempt — two attempts are usually allowed for in pre-study planning. This approach can be described in 'pseudo-mathematics' as DN + 3 + 1 + 1, illustrating the stages in optimization.

Throughout the option development and optimization process it is absolutely essential to bear in mind the inter-relationship of the components, and indeed of individual schemes. Taken to extremes, it is obvious, for example, that a park-and-ride system without adequate and attractive 'ride' facilities is destined to failure — as also might it be if adequate parking facilities were simultaneously available nearer the central area.

The Continual Process

It is too much to hope that the resultant preferred strategy is the definitive best strategy for the area under study. It can only be an approximation, with the inevitable built-in bias of the options investigated and the subjective weighting of evaluation results. But the choice of the preferred strategy — which is, in any case, a matter for political decision, based on technical advice — is not a final, irreversible matter. It is only the direction in which the actual programmed policies and schemes will move until the strategy is reviewed in the light of later developments. Within 5 to 10 years the whole process will almost certainly need review, but at shorter intervals minor reviews and monitoring exercises should also be undertaken. Transport planning is a continuing process — the development of a preferred strategy is not a once-and-for-all-time exercise.

SUMMARY

a) Transportation study results can only be as good as the options considered. The 'building' of the initial options is therefore of very great importance.

b) The base for comparison of the alternative options is the Do-nothing (DN) or Economic Base strategy, which has to be made a viable alternative.

c) The DN strategy, in common with all others, is built of a mix of public transport services, restraint policies and optimum use of existing and new roads.

d) The sketch-plan approach to option development is recommended, attention being given to the balance of the various expenditure measures, both capital and recurrent, and revenue.

e) Optimization, inevitably to some extent a subjective process, is unlikely to determine the definitive best strategy — all that can be hoped for is that this will be approached, and long-term mistakes avoided.

9

The Assessment of Urban Transportation Options

The prime objective of any type of urban transportation study is, as already emphasized, the development of an optimum comprehensive strategy. This development is achieved as a result of the comparative assessment of largely subjectively developed alternatives. The comparative assessment is carried out in as objective a manner as possible but eventually, in common with all parts of the transport planning process, is of course subject to political decision, reflecting the public's view of desirability and/or acceptability. Political over-riding aside however, the task of the comprehensive transport planner is to compare sensible alternatives on a uniform basis and advise the decision-makers of the quantifiable facts.

The methods open to the transport planner for the assessment of urban options are basically those of operational and environmental assessment and economic evaluation. There is of course a measure of overlapping of benefits across these processes, which also vary considerably in their sophistication. And perhaps more important, there are also many gaps in the assessment process, such as the assessment of benefits or disbenefits to the non-travelling public, most assessment techniques being based on transport-user benefits. But the defects in the available processes could not be considered as justification for ignoring their considerable usefulness — as long as the results are interpreted with common sense and are not accepted blindly.

Because the object of the exercise must be to obtain the best overall value for the public moneys expended, it would perhaps not be unreasonable for the economic evaluation process to at least be considered as the 'senior partner'. In an ideal situation, this view would be acceptable, and indeed, if *all* benefits and disbenefits were quantifiable, *only* an economic evaluation would perhaps be needed — but this is not yet so. In present-day conditions and with presently available techniques the transport planner has to fall back on subjective relating of a variety of different assessment criteria. Nevertheless, if only because of its more complete quantification, the economic evaluation process inevitably attracts greater weight in any consideration. After all, money is a 'scarce resource', to use economists' jargon.

Operational Assessment

Looking at operational assessment first, however — because of its slightly earlier application in the optimization process and also perhaps because of its longer-established though 'woolier' assessment method — this is a measure of *effectiveness*, irrespective of cost. Operational assessment, which is largely geared to highway systems, has a useful role, in both option development and at the final optimization stages, in identifying trouble-spots or pinchpoints in a system. Once options have been built and optimized, operational assessment techniques also afford readily assimilated, diagrammatically presentable, criteria for non-professional system comparison.

The prime basis of conventional operational assessment of highway networks is the comparison of traffic flow with road capacity — the volume : capacity (V/C) ratio. Comparing links of two single-carriageway roads, each carrying a predicted peak-hour design-year two-way flow of say 1000 vehicles per hour, one road's capacity might be say 500 vph and the other, slightly wider and with better junctions, might be 1000 vph. The volume : capacity ratios would clearly be 2·0 and 1·0 respectively, reflecting the ineffectiveness of the narrower road.

In that situation, looking at two roads of basically similar characteristics, the V/C ratio is a valid comparison of the relative effectiveness of the two links. It is less use however in comparing the effectiveness of a single-carriageway road with a dual carriageway. Although a dual carriageway may be as crowded, or over-loaded, as a single carriageway, the demands made on driver skill and concentration are less, as also is the rate of speed reduction due to increased flow. To compensate for these variables, the somewhat arbitrary level-of-service criterion is sometimes used as a measure of operational effectiveness. In this way, levels of service throughout a whole network of roads can be uniformly compared.

In the *Strategic Plan for the South East* (of England), consultants R. Travers Morgan & Partners defined levels of service (A,B,C, etc.).

Road type	Design capacity pcu/h	Flow levels (pcu/h) for level of service group				
		A/B	C/D	E	F	F*
Motorway	1000/lane	<1000	1001–1650	1651–2000	2001–2800	>2800
All purpose dual	1000/lane	< 850	851–1350	1351–1650	1651–2400	>2400
Good single	1200 (*2-way*)	< 900	901–1700	1701–2000	2001–3600	>3600
Poor single	800 (*2-way*)	< 400	401– 900	901–1100	1101–2400	>2400

Just as the V/C ratios can be determined for each link in a road network, so too can a similar measure be derived for selected junctions in a network. And although a more complicated calculation, this is perhaps of greater importance, for it is the capacity of a junction that largely determines the adequacy of adjacent links. Because of the more involved computation however, only a limited number of junctions are usually assessed in this way.

As well as these measures of localized congestion it is customary also to determine such overall criteria as overall average trip length (or often, trip cost) and average journey speeds. Together with global values of these indicators, they can usefully also be determined on a sectoral, temporal, or purpose basis.

While these latter criteria are relatively easily determined by computer, their interpretation is less straightforward; and the system-wide criterion may be of questionable validity — a good overall index may well hide extremely bad but very localized features. The localized congestion measures however are of particular use when developing options, after an initial model-run has been assigned to eliminate bottlenecks. For presentation to non-professional decision-makers, the link V/C ratios can be computer-plotted on a band-width basis — preferably with V/C ratios pre-grouped — superimposed on a spider road network for identification.

While, as already explained, the majority of operational assessment criteria have been primarily developed for highway network appraisal, it is not impossible to develop similar criteria relating to the public-transport network. This sort of criteria has seldom been used in the past — earlier urban transportation studies being somewhat lacking in their public transport content — but such link measures as non-seated-passengers or total-network-passenger-distance are currently being considered, along with the obvious average-passenger trip length and/or cost.

For the visual presentation of both private and public transport comparative operational effectiveness however, perhaps the most useful technique is the use of a form of contour map. A few selected major trip attractors, such as shopping areas, major work-places, etc., can be chosen and contours of generalized costs and/or peak travel times from these attractors by alternative modes can be superimposed on the map base. Off-peak costs/times would perhaps be more appropriate for some attractors. Together with and derived from these visual presentations, it is helpful also to determine the population within a specific cost/time distance from, say, work-places or shopping areas. Other than on this accessibility basis, present operational assessment methods do not permit the comparison of one mode with another.

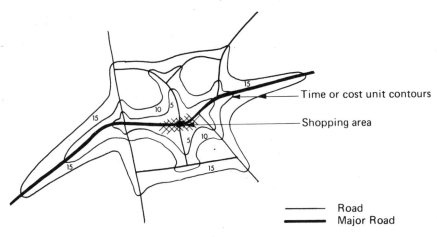

Fig. 9.1 Accessibility contours

Economic Evaluation

As already pointed out, all methods of operational assessment ignore the cost constraint, merely measuring the effectiveness of various uni-modal systems rather than the more important *cost-effectiveness* or efficiency of a whole comprehensive transport system. When, however, several options are each developed to utilize the whole of a common total amount of resources, this omission becomes of less importance, although there is still the inability to compare across modes. To measure the overall cost-effectiveness of comprehensive urban transport plans the economic evaluation process is essential. The use of the term evaluation is justified by the more fully quantified nature of the economic tests compared with the somewhat more subjective nature of most operational and environmental assessments.

Economic evaluation of urban transport systems, in common with most non-commercial undertakings, involves the determination of some form of benefit : cost ratio, rather than the profit : cost ratio appropriate to the business world. And the benefits in urban areas are customarily measured in terms of generalized cost savings. But, as we have already seen, the generalized costs used in the trip distribution process are based on the drivers' perception of his journey cost and are not necessarily the 'correct' valuation. These behavioural costs do not allow for such matters as taxation either — fuel tax payment is not a true use of resources. For evaluation purposes therefore, different, 'correct', generalized costs are used, with compensation for the effect of the true resources costs being incorporated.

The method by which variations in user benefits across different transport systems are measured is known as the *consumer surplus* approach, a particular characteristic of which is the allowance for variation in the number of i-j trips made. Well-known to economists, the demand curve/consumer surplus concept is perhaps less commonplace to other transport planning disciplines, meriting therefore a simple explanation.

Fig. 9.2 Consumer surplus/demand curve concept

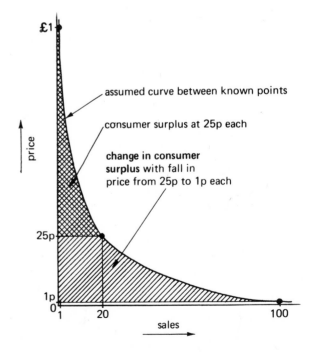

assumed curve between known points

consumer surplus at 25p each

change in consumer surplus with fall in price from 25p to 1p each

Think of a very rich man who, perhaps for health reasons, has to eat an apple a day. Being rich he alone might well be prepared to pay £1 for an apple if they were very scarce. Consider now a doting husband whose pregnant wife was craving for an apple. For peace of mind he might just be prepared to pay 25p for an apple. So might some other poeple — say 20 people in all. Finally, consider the many prudent housewives who, when apples are 1p each will buy a lot for bottling — say 100 people. If the one sale at £1, the 20 sales at 25p and the 100 sales at 1p are plotted and connected, the resultant line is referred to as a demand curve.

When apples are 25p each the man willing to pay £1 for his apple will have a surplus, or notional saving, of 75p. Similarly, the odd person willing to pay less than £1 but more than 25p will also be making a saving, or surplus, but of less magnitude. The total surplus made by all the consumers is the area beneath the curve above the 25p horizontal. If now the price of apples fell to 1p, at that price the consumer surplus would be the area beneath the curve above the 1p horizontal. The more important *change* in consumer surplus between the two prices is the area bounded by the two price horizontals, the vertical axis and the curve.

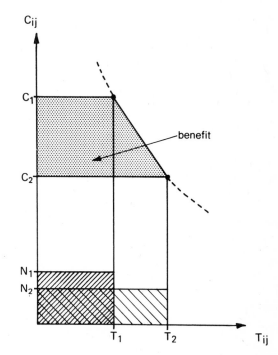

Fig. 9.3 Consumer surplus and resource element for i − j trips

Applying this concept to urban movement, consider the total number of trips from zone i to zone j. From the transportation study process we have determined that in the Do-nothing system with an interzonal generalized cost of C_{ij1} there will be T_{ij1} trips made, and that in one of the alternative options, because of a lower journey cost C_{ij2}, there will be such trip *redistribution* that there will be T_{ij2} trips made.

Note that it is redistribution, i.e. a changed trip destination, not a trip generation, which would require an additional trip leaving zone i (which cannot be allowed for in this approach). We do not know the actual consumer surplus at either trip cost but we do now know the two most important points on the demand curve. From an assumption that the demand curve is sensibly a straight line between these points the change in consumer surplus can be calculated. It is:

$$\tfrac{1}{2}(T_{ij1} + T_{ij2})(C_{ij1} - C_{ij2})$$

To correct for the non-resource element within that formula, letting N_1 and N_2 be that element, $(N_2 T_{ij2} - N_1 T_{ij1})$ should be added, i.e.:

$$\text{Movement benefit} \atop \text{for } i-j \text{ trips} = \tfrac{1}{2}(T_{ij1} + T_{ij2})(C_{ij1} - C_{ij2}) + (N_2 T_{ij2} - N_1 T_{ij1})$$

This change in consumer surplus is then totalled over all modes, all ij pairs, all purposes, all time groupings etc., to give the total movement benefit of a Do-something option over the DN system. Remember that many social benefits have been ignored in this calculation.

(By algebraic manipulation, which need not be repeated here, the formula can be rewritten and expanded to become, for a whole system:

Total movement benefit equals

$$\tfrac{1}{2} \Sigma (u_1 - u_2)(q_1 + q_2) + \Sigma(q_2 u_2 - q_1 u_1) - \Sigma(q_2 r_2 - q_1 r_1) - \Delta T \frac{\phi_n}{\phi_t}$$

where Σ allows for summation over all ij pairs, modes, purposes, etc.

$u_1 u_2$ = behavioural generalized $i - j$ costs allowing for society's valuation of time

$q_1 q_2$ = T_{ij1}, T_{ij2}

$r_1 r_2$ = unit resource costs, i.e. excluding indirect taxation

ΔT = increase in tax paid on transport

$\phi_t \phi_n$ = taxation rates in transport sector and in remainder of economy.)

Having ascertained the total year's movement benefit of one of the optional systems over the Economic Base or DN system in the design year (taken, as usual, as 1991) and deducted all related increased annual costs to derive the net benefits, this can be related to the total cost of the new system in excess of the unavoidable expenditure on the DN system. Expressed as a percentage (benefits/cost) this ratio is a single-year-system economic rate of return. Note that it is not a first-year rate of return as often used in inter-urban scheme assessments.

Because of the variable (from town to town) and unquantified benefits (positive or negative) to the non-travelling public which are excluded from the economic evaluation process, and from the study-specific factors incorporated in the process, the single-year system rate of return is not suitable for comparing strategies in one town with those in another town, nor for comparison with other public-sector investments. The rate of return is only a means of ranking alternatives within the town to which they relate. Furthermore, because of the omissions from the method, and also particularly because the benefits are small differences between large amounts — and therefore over-sensitive — the rates of return should not be taken as absolute criteria.

NOTE

There is an increasing awareness that, for the comparative appraisal of strategies operating at different levels of efficiency — e.g. with less than the maximum possible use of the available infrastructure — and with different levels of *capital* expenditure, the determination of a single-year rate of return is inappropriate. A better approach is now thought to be a descriptive appraisal of the benefits attributable to each strategy and of the incremental benefits due to specific investments or policies.

It is inappropriate to assume, for example, that a system with a 12·9% rate of return is better than one with a 12·8% rate — the method is too crude to assume other than that both systems are equally suitable.

There are many valid objections to the use of a single-year 'snapshot' of benefits for evaluation purposes. It would be far better to compare alternative strategies on a *net present value* basis over perhaps 30 years, as is increasingly done for inter-urban scheme evaluation. To arrive at the net present value (NPV) of an urban system it is necessary to determine the annual costs and benefits in each of the next thirty years, and having discounted all to a 'present year', sum them, taking benefits as positive and costs as negative.

Even using a key-year approach (at 5-year intervals) and interpolating for intermediate years, the NPV method entails many more transportation model runs which are not as yet a financial possibility. Furthermore, the need to consider intermediate years inevitably leads to the desirability of both across-the-board part-system comparisons and within-systems phasing comparisons at each key year — increasing study costs very considerably. There is little doubt that a move towards NPV urban system evaluation is inevitable, but it will almost certainly be a very limited adoption, based on broad assumptions.

Lastly, on the subject of the economic evaluation, it is important always to remember the significant omissions from the quantified benefits. And among the most important of the excluded social considerations are the effects of traffic noise, visual intrusion, and other environmental aspects. These effects are considered separately — in an environmental assessment.

Environmental Assessment

There has been, in many countries, increasing public concern in recent years over the disadvantageous environmental effects of transport policies and their implementation. Benefit to the relatively few motorists is no longer considered as outweighing or even balancing the adverse effects on everybody's way of life. More and more, individual road schemes are being specifically designed — or redesigned — to reduce their environmental impact. But this is not enough. The environmental effects of transport policies spread far beyond the mere surroundings of a specific urban scheme — they are felt throughout the urban area as travel demands are changed, traffic redistributed, and so on. Environmental matters need to be considered at overall transport strategy level; the strategies themselves need to be chosen with due regard to the overall environmental consequences.

Unlike the operational and economic appraisal methods, which although continually developing, have in general, been used in many transport studies and are widely accepted, the environmental assessment methods are still at an early stage in development and acceptance. The factors involved in environmental considerations, however, are generally agreed to include:

traffic noise
visual intrusion
pollution by traffic fumes
pedestrian/vehicle conflict (pedestrian delays)

severance

land take

and methods are at various stages of development for quantifying in one form or another several of these effects. Some effects, however, can still be assessed only on a purely subjective basis.

Because of lack of value consistency as yet in financial evaluation, and of meaningless subjectivity in any form of weighted-scores evaluation, environmental evaluation is at present usually undertaken on the basis of separate appraisal of each of the quantifiable factors. The problem with this approach is the combining together of the measured impacts of different environmental factors — the trade-offs. This is a matter which is left to the politicians — the decision-makers.

Of the factors listed above, it is usually accepted that the most important and most readily quantifiable ones are noise, visual intrusion, pedestrian delays, and land-take, broadly in that order. The remaining factors are usually considered in a purely subjective appraisal.

For environmental appraisal purposes noise is measured in terms of the 18-hour L_{10} noise levels, in dB(A) units. The L_{10} value is the noise level which is exceeded for 10 per cent of the time, (and similarly, the sometimes mentioned L_{50} and L_{90} values are levels exceeded for 50 and 90 per cent of the time) and is usually related to an (18-hour) average hour between 0600 and 2400. dB(A) units are decibels, as measured directly by a sound meter, but these are then factored, or weighted by a scale A to correspond to the subjective impression of loudness as heard through the human ear. In these units, an increase of 10 dB(A) is approximately equivalent to doubling the loudness.

In order to predict 18-hour L_{10} values for future traffic noise, various forumlae have been developed in respect of free-flow and non-free-flow traffic conditions, which relate mean traffic speed, traffic flow, and the percentage of heavy vehicles in the traffic stream to the noise level. These formulae are usually incorporated in computer programs but when used manually are often expressed as a family of curves. It is not in fact necessary to actually measure or predict the traffic flows over an 18-hour period — it has been found that the peak-hour L_{10} value, less 3 dB(A), is a reasonable approximation.

But the basic formulae only predict traffic noise at a reference distance — often 10 metres — from the traffic stream. An equally important calculation is the determination of the attenuation of this noise — how it falls off with distance away from the reference point near the road in different circumstances and with differing obstacles or noise barriers. Again, families of curves permit the assessment of these effects, and as a result it is possible to plot noise contours on large-scale network maps. From the noise contours relating to alternative transport systems, the numbers of households experiencing different noise levels can be determined and used as a measure of environmental effect. Where the facade of a dwelling experiences 18-hour L_{10} noise levels exceeding 70 dB(A) double glazing is almost certainly necessary.

The visual intrusion of new road structures elevated above ground-level is also something of considerable impact, for which a quantified appraisal approach has been developed. The visual impact is measured in terms of the solid angle subtended by a new structure from a given observation point, in units of *steradians*. A steradian is defined as the angle subtended at the centre of a sphere of unit radius by unit area of the surface, the total solid angle around any point being 4π steradians. Tentatively, until public visual reactions have been assessed, solid angles have been grouped and classified as slight, noticeable, and marked, visual intrusion. Within these categories, the total numbers of households in a strategy affected by the degrees of visual intrusion are determined and compared with numbers for other strategies.

One way of determining the solid angle subtended by a new structure is for it to be plotted on a 'fish-eye' or $180°$ field photograph of the structure-less location and the solid angle determined by a simple process of counting squares on a transparent overlay, specially designed for the relevant photographic field. More usually, a planimeter-like solid-angle calculator, calibrated to a standard plan scale, can be used on a plan of the new structure, taking separate account of the approximate height of the structure above ground level.

Apart from the visual intrusion of a new road structure, there is the very real visual intrusion of the road traffic itself, which is not allowed for in the above method. This intrusion obviously occurs as much, if not more, as a result of traffic on roads at ground level as it does from traffic on elevated structures. There is as yet no generally accepted technique for the measurement of an equivalent solid angle for the moving traffic — and it might therefore be appropriate for this factor to be included or allowed for in a later subjective appraisal.

Delays to pedestrians due to traffic presence, another environmental consideration, occur mainly in congested shopping streets and can be predicted as a funtion of traffic volume and speed, road width and crossing facilities, and pedestrian age. Numbers of road-crossing pedestrians can be approximately determined from data on shopping floor space per road network link, and applied to the average delay prediction. By summing the pedestrian-hours of delay per day for all relevant links in a network, a measure of overall network delay can then be ascertained, and compared with other strategies.

With the greater concern for the environmental consequences of new urban road construction, the approach to road design will often now be such that additional land needs to be acquired, beyond that needed strictly for construction purposes. This additional land-take, which is measured and compared across alternative strategies, will provide for such environmental requirements as sound barriers or mounds, and the purchase of land or dwellings blighted by the new road. Provision should also be made for the purchase of small parcels of land no longer usable because of their reduced size.

Combining Appraisal Results

Should the results of operational assessment, economic evaluation and the several environmental assessment techniques all indicate a clear preference for a particular strategy, the transport planner would probably die of shock. This is too much to expect — and in fact could well indicate a poor and over-restricted choice of alternatives. More likely might be a set of criteria of the following form:

	System A	System B	System C
Total cost	£15·1m	£14·9m	£15·3m
Net economic benefits (compared with DN)	£154 000	£155 000	£169 000
Economic evaluation: Single-year rate of return	10·2% (3)	10·4% (2)	11·1% (1)
Operational assessment ranking	(1)	(3)	(2)
Environmental assessment: (all compared with DN) Noise: No. of dwellings needing double-glazing	250 (2)	300 (3)	200 (1)
Noise: No. of dwellings 5 dB(A) worse	200 (1)	250 (2)	250 (2)
VI: No. of dwellings with marked intrusion	40 (2)	30 (1)	50 (3)
Pedestrian delay (hrs)	28 (2)	30 (3)	25 (1)
Land-take (hA)	28 (1)	40 (3)	30 (2)
Overall environmental ranking	(1)	(3)	(2)

(Figures in brackets indicate ranking for that specific criterion)

Looking first at the environmental criteria, there can be little doubt that System B is the least preferable system. System A seems to be slightly preferable to System C, not being the worst on any count, but the choice is clearly marginal. On the overall assessment therefore the rankings can be summarized:

	A	B	C
Economic	3	2	1
Operational	1	3	2
Environmental	1	3	2

The choice is clearly between systems A and C, C being preferred on economic grounds and A on other counts. It is then a question of assessing whether the operational and environmental benefits of system A are worth the sacrifice of the £15 000 (£169 000 − £154 000) of annual benefit. The £15 000 annual benefits are bought at an additional capital cost of £0·2m (£15·3m − £15·1m), indicating only a 7½ per cent incremental rate of return — which is decidedly marginal. It is appropriate to indicate again the degree of scepticism that should be applied to results such as these. To state categorically that an 11·1% rate of return was significantly better than 10·4% and 10·2% is difficult — it is probably just about significant. Certainly the difference between 10·4% and 10·2% is of very little significance at all. It must be remembered that the benefits are derived from the *differences* of two large user-cost calculations — slight errors in the user cost calculations cause major differences in the benefits.

To set against the economic benefits, however, the major environmental disbenefits amount to 50 dwellings exposed to an additional

5 dB(A) and 10 dwellings with greater visual intrusion. A decision needs to be made as to whether these disbenefits are worth something like £15 000 per year — and this will probably depend on the quality of the affected dwellings. The basis of any such recommendation made by the transport planner must be clearly explained to the political decision-makers, whose decision, founded on their feel for the general public's requirements and preferences, may reverse the planner's recommendation.

Should the whole question of choice of a transport strategy be set before the general public, for a participative sounding of public opinion, it is sensible to give as many of the facts as possible, and an indication of official preference. These facts should include assessment results such as those tabulated above, in order that the effects of possible changes can be fully appreciated. Following any such public-participation exercise it is desirable that a final decision be made as soon as possible, to avoid blight on properties affected by rejected strategies.

To undertake a public-participation exercise without making provision for taking account of the public's views will almost certainly lead to failure; but the public should be approached with a preferred strategy and the reasons for the preference. These seemingly conflicting requirements can be resolved in the 'DN + 3 + 1 + 1' approach mentioned earlier by ascertaining the public's views after the first optimization run and incorporating their views in the final run. This could be expressed as 'DN + 3 + 1 + PP + 1' — PP indicating public participation.

Longer-term Strategy Appraisal

The assessment methods described so far in this chapter have all been relevant to the appraisal of medium-term (1991) alternative strategies, based on a single land-use input. When the transport aspects of longer-term (end-of-century) plans — which will cover alternative land uses as well as other, vaguer policies — are considered, not all of these methods are appropriate. Because of the variable land-use input the consumer-surplus approach to economic evaluation is not acceptable — and no comparably simple method is at present available. Similarly, to undertake a quantified environmental appraisal as far ahead as the end of the century smacks of spurious accuracy — particularly as the results are somewhat arbitrary even at the medium-term date. The basic method of appraisal of long-term transport plans is therefore the long-established one of operational assessment — and even then, mainly as a guide to what is largely a subjective comparison.

Given an optimized and robust medium-term transport plan, however, and a reasonably fixed-capital transport budget, it is unlikely that transport considerations will have a significant effect on the choice of long-term land use disposition. Basically, within the constraints mentioned, a broadly comparable transport strategy can be developed to suit almost any sensible land-use plan. The long-term land-use disposition is more likely to be based on non-transport considerations — water supply or sewerage possibilities, agricultural values etc. The important pre-requisite is just that the medium-term transport plan be 'robust', i.e. flexible enough not to preclude desirable long-term dispositions.

SUMMARY

a) The main assessment methods for urban transport strategies are operational assessment, economic evaluation and environmental assessment.

b) The basic criterion for operational assessment, which measures the effectiveness of the system, is the volume : capacity ratio and its more subjective derivation, the level of service. Both of these measures are readily displayed pictorially for lay appreciation. Accessibility contours, which can also be displayed on maps, are another useful form of operational assessment.

c) Economic evaluation of urban transport systems is based on a consumer surplus approach measuring the changing generalized cost of journeys, but is not capable of assessing the value of generated traffic. A net-present-value approach to economic evaluation, while undoubtedly desirable, is probably too expensive for early adoption.

d) Environmental assessment of urban systems on a quantified basis is virtually restricted to prediction of noise, visual intrusion, and pedestrian delay effects, plus the comparison of alternative land-takes.

e) The combination of the several assessment methods usually involves a trade-off procedure which must inevitably be highly subjective — the assumptions made therein should therefore be drawn to the attention of the political decision-makers.

f) Longer-term strategy appraisal depends almost entirely on operational assessment methods. The most important requirement is for robust medium-term strategy from which the longer-term strategy can be developed.

10

The Smaller Urban Area

So far, much of our attention has been directed to the problems of the large urban area. This is entirely appropriate in view of the greater importance and transport impact of these problems within the overall transport system. But what of the other urban areas — the smaller towns without such special justifications for the transportation study approach as major development changes or rapidly expanding population? There are many such ordinary towns in any national, regional or county context.

The smaller town — and we can perhaps visualize a typical town as being one of about 30 000 population — has transport problems, but they are different from those of the large town. The solutions too are different. And because of its size, the capital resources likely to be available for transport investment in a small town, within a typical planning period, are also small — possibly less than proportionately so.

The Pre-planning Process

The overall investigation and broad planning process however is equally appropriate to the small town as to the large one. The prime requirement is for facts — facts on present problems and sensible projections of future problems. With a feel for the problems, alternative solutions can be postulated and appraised before the selection of what is, hopefully, the optimum solution. The main differences are in the form of the future prediction and the availability of possible remedies for the different types of problem.

In the small urban area it is possible to acquire some preliminary feel for the problems by a comprehensive look at the present situation — by visiting the known centres of congestion at peak periods, by studying the queues at major junctions, and at bus stops. Together with this physical investigation, a desk exercise can readily be undertaken on any available traffic flow information, and most towns have at least some traffic counts or survey data.

The object of the 'pre-think' process is to make some assessment of the type of transport study that is or will be necessary. And it is important to bear in mind that the objective is to plan a good, practical transport system — not necessarily to undertake a sophisticated study. With the smaller town, it may be that a significant part of the central urban congestion is due to through traffic. From a number of origin and destination surveys undertaken in Britain in the early 1960s it can be postulated that around 40 per cent of traffic *approaching*, i.e. not in, a town of 30 000 population is 'bypassable' — *Urban Traffic Engineering Techniques,* HMSO, 1965. In these conditions, a basically

inter-urban type bypass might be a solution — at least, one worth
considering alongside perhaps a town-centre relief road. If nothing
else, this possibility would indicate that a tight urban study would not
suffice but that a study geared to the appraisal of the bypass might be
more appropriate.

The 'pre-think' process will also identify the availability of options.
Specifically, if a town has an established plan to build an inner relief
road, of which the first two parts of a three-part construction phasing
are either complete or in hand, it may well be that there is little
alternative to completing the relief road. And because of the limited
financial resources, the final stage may be all the capital works that
can be undertaken in the period under review.

Small-Town Option Restriction

But prior construction commitments and financial resources are not
the only constraints on available options in the small urban area. The
options that are available in large urban areas for major new public
transport systems — perhaps based on segregated track, such as busways
etc., or significantly extended and improved existing services — are not
usually appropriate. Bus services in smaller towns are frequently
dominated by through or inter-town services provided by the county
operator, routeing and frequency being, to some extent, a function of
out-of-town destination rather than within-town need. The population
of the small town is seldom large enough to warrant the high quality
bus service that is needed to induce modal-choice changes.

Conversely of course, traffic congestion in the smaller town is
usually considerably less than in the large town. It may be unpleasant
and cause delay to both within-town commuters and to through traffic,
but is most unlikely to extend over a large area of the town or over a
long period of the day. Indeed, it may be that the problem in some
towns is so minor that there is little need to do anything at all to
relieve it.

At the same time, with this less serious congestion and limited scope
for improved public transport, there is less need and less freedom to
impose any significant restraint on the private car. The overall quantity
of travel is not markedly elastic and if no more attractive alternative
mode can be offered, restraint on the car is unlikely to be either
readily enforceable or effective. In the smaller town it is often more
appropriate to control parking and the locations of car parks than to
restrict the availability. It is, of course, fundamental that all existing
road space should be available for the movement of people and goods —
in moving vehicles — and not pre-empted by stationary, parked vehicles.

Traffic Management

Within the small-town financial and modal-choice inducement constraints
mentioned above it is often realistic to plan only on the implementation
of traffic management measures. One measure is the restriction — if not
the abolition — of on-street parking, but it must be remembered that
the juxtaposition of a fee-charging, commercially-oriented off-street
car park with readily available, free or low-cost on-street parking spaces

is economically non-viable. The off-street park will of course be under-utilized, while the streets are cluttered up with congestion-causing parked vehicles. Other measures appropriate to the small town include particularly:
a) pedestrianization, particularly of central shopping streets, often linked with
b) one-way systems, permitting the avoidance (and pedestrianization) of the central shopping area, but often at the expense of the environmental qualities of streets receiving the diverted traffic.

Also in the small town at least as much emphasis as in the larger urban area should be placed on the preservation of the environmental quality of town life when planning traffic-management systems. Road safety considerations too must be taken into account, particularly as traffic-receiving streets in a small town are likely to have previously been relatively quieter than those in the large towns. And where one-way systems, street closures, etc. have been adopted it is of equal importance to ensure that through-routes are adequately signposted — remembering the larger proportion of through traffic in the small town than in the large town.

Alternative Study Processes

Traffic management measures aside however, there will still remain in many small urban areas, some, albeit probably limited, need for the provision of new roads. And depending on the likely need for such provision and the predictable pattern of the town's development, there are basically three appropriate study processes. These are:
a) a small, relatively simple, yet conventional, transportation study,
b) a growth-factor type exercise, such as that based on the Furness procedure,
c) a basically desk exercise of simply grossing up measured traffic flows, possibly with manual, subjective, adjustments.

There are available one or two computer program packages providing material for conventional and somewhat standardized urban transportation studies to be undertaken at relatively low cost. The best known of these packages is the COMPACT 2 program, which is basically a distribution and modal split model with all-or-nothing assignment output. COMPACT 2 offers a conventional generalized cost-based two-mode gravity model, sometimes appropriate to the small town which has problems of significant land-use or population-distribution changes, or needs to look at the choice of alternative modes. It does not include a trip-generation procedure; trip ends therefore have to be predetermined by an 'outside' routine, and input to COMPACT 2. A further major aspect inhibiting COMPACT 2's use by inexperienced operators is the still-present need for the model to be calibrated — which can, as always, be very time- and cost-consuming. Accepting these restrictions however, COMPACT 2 probably offers a reasonable means of predicting small-town future travel patterns where the expected changes are such as to warrant its use.

The simple, iteratively-balanced growth-factor type of study, such as that based on the Furness approach, is often admirably suited to the problems of the small town. It enables due account to be taken of

---

COMPACT 2 — A Simplified Program for Transportation Studies

COMPACT 2 can build networks, i.e. determine 'trees', distribute trips, determine modal split, and assign person- or vehicle-trips to networks.

COMPACT 2 permits a study area of a maximum of 98 zones and a network of not more than 135 nodes and 540 links to be studied. Journeys are modelled from 2-person-type trip-end data to give a choice of 2 modes for up to 6 trip-purposes.

COMPACT 2 requires link data to be input in terms of distance, and time or speed, from which generalized cost characteristics are internally computed.

COMPACT 2 is based on a gravity model incorporating a choice of trip-cost deterrence function, of either exponential, negative power, or combined gamma (Tanner) form.

COMPACT 2 distribution may be selected to be either singly or doubly constrained, i.e. to ensure either only that $\Sigma_j T_{ij} = G_i$ or that the second constraint, $\Sigma_i T_{ij} = A_j$ is also met.

COMPACT 2 requires trip-end data to be input.

COMPACT 2 does not include an economic evaluation routine, and output matrices need to be externally manipulated to provide data for such a calculation, although this is relatively straightforward.

COMPACT 2 uses simple, clearly defined inputs and provides a small but adequate range of useful outputs in a program that can, by virtue of its size restriction and integrated design, quickly and cheaply be run to completion, without the need for intermediate output inspection and control.

---

variations in zonal growth and permits the reassignment of trips to improved routes. Its major defects are its inability to model the *redistributive* effect of new transport facilities and the inability to model changes in modal split other than by inputting intuitive proportions. But, while these deficiencies are of great importance in the large urban area, they are of little significance in the smaller town and the growth factor approach may often be applied with confidence.

Basically, the investigation area, i.e. the town alone or together with sufficient hinterland to encompass possible bypasses, is divided into zones as for a conventional study. An origin and destination trip matrix by mode is determined for the present, or base, year — either from household interviews or from screen line and cordon roadside interviews. Zonal growth factors are then determined to predict the design year (1991) generations and attractions for each zone, taking account of population changes, car-ownership rates, real-income variations, land-use changes, etc. These zonal growth factors are then applied to the total Gs and As to give a future-year matrix of correct totals but base-year cell figures. These cell figures are then factored in turn, horizontally and vertically, to produce a balanced future-trip matrix by the specified mode. The resultant T_{ij} cell figures can then be assigned by one of the

Growth Factor Distribution — the Furness Approach

Consider a three-zone model, with an observed, base-year matrix as shown at matrix (a). On the basis of predicted zonal land-use changes, car-ownership growth, etc., the generations and attractions in each zone at a future date are determined and applied to the row and column totals, resulting in the G (generations) and A (attractions) total figures shown in matrix (b). The row- and column-factors are applied and recalculated alternately as demonstrated in matrix (b) until both the row- and column-totals can be accepted as adequately balanced, i.e. within about 2 or 3 per cent. Consider cell T_{1-2}: The 20 trips in matrix (a) are multiplied by the basic zonal factor of 1·5 relating to zone 1 generations, to give the first figure in the matrix (b) cell of 30. When this zone 2 column is summed vertically the A total is 60 compared with the required 60, indicating a new factor of 1·0 (60/60). When this is applied the T_{12} figure remains at 30, the second figure in matrix (b). Summed horizontally now, the G_1 total is 44 giving a third factor of 1·14 ... and so on.

A\G	ZONE 1	ZONE 2	ZONE 3	TOTAL	GRTH. FACT. 1
ZONE 1	–	20	13	33	1.5
ZONE 2	5	–	12	17	3.0
ZONE 3	35	15	–	50	2.0
TOTAL	40	35	25	100	
GRTH. FACT.	2.5	1.7	1.6		

Matrix (a) being base year movements — but with overall zonal growth factors to design year indicated outside of row and column totals

Matrix (b) being design year cell flows and showing calculation stages in deriving these flows

A\G	1	2	3	G	TOT. 2	FACT. 3	TOT. 4	FACT. 5	TOT. 6	
1	–	30 30 34 33 35 34	20 14 16 14 15 14	50	44	1.14	47	1.07	48	
2	15 18 20 22 23 24	–	36 26 30 26 27 26	50	44	1.14	48	1.04	50	Accept
3	70 82 73 78 74 76	30 30 27 27 26 25	–	100	112	0.9	105	0.96	101	
A	100	60	40	200						

	1	2	3
TOT. 1	85	60	56
FACT. 2	1.18	1.00	0.72
TOT. 3	93	61	46
FACT. 4	1.07	0.98	0.87
TOT. 5	97	61	42
FACT. 6	1.03	0.99	0.95

Key to cell figure order

1	2
3	4
5	6

techniques previously described — or perhaps adequately by the diversion curve approach — to obtain actual future link flows.

The other, even simpler, approach to future traffic prediction is based firmly on measured existing traffic flows on the road network, the measurement consisting of actual manual or automatic counting of peak-hour or all-day flow figures on each significant link in the road network. The same approach can also be applied to simple OD survey data developed to form desire-line flows. The observed link or desire-line flows are factored by a single, area-wide multiplier representing predictable growth from base year to design year. Totally inappropriate to the larger urban area where zonal changes are inevitably more variable, this approach may be acceptable in the small town, where overall income growth and car-ownership increases are more significant than other factors. The growth factors could either be locally determined, based on known regional trends, or merely the standard, national Tanner factors (see Chapter 2 for Tanner factors). Clearly the common growth-factor approach makes no allowance for localized area growth differences, but if a particular sector of a town is to be differentially developed, then it is possible for the design-year factored flows to be manually adjusted — subjectively — with all the susceptibility to challenge that that approach involves.

Option Development

No matter which prediction approach is adopted for the small town, there remains — as in all other areas of comprehensive transport planning — the need to use the predicted demands to compare alternative, similar-cost solutions to the problems. With the small-scale transportation study approach the design-year options would be developed and appraised in the same way as for a larger town, i.e. each option involving a redistribution of trips. With the Furness zonal growth factor process or the simple, single-factor approach however, each option will be based on the same, fixed matrix of inter-zonal trips. This fixed matrix means that the only differences between options are in the actual routes adopted by the future flows, i.e. merely an assignment differential.

Notwithstanding this inherent defect — which is of course of less importance in the small town than it would be in the larger town — it is necessary that alternative options are assessed by comparison with a DN option, as for the large town.

Option Assessment

The assessment methods should be basically the same as for the large towns, i.e. operational, economic and environmental, but with a fixed matrix there is no need for a consumer-surplus approach to the economic evaluation. There are no extra trips between i and j, diverted from other destinations; only journey cost savings resulting from improved networks. In this situation the simpler approach can be adopted, based on

$$\text{Overall benefit} = \Sigma T_{ij}(C_{ij1} - C_{ij2})$$

where
Σ allows for summation over all ij pairs, modes, purposes etc.
T_{ij} = trips from i to j
C_{ij1}, C_{ij2} = respectively, 'before' and 'after' trip costs from i to j.
The usual method of actual calculation of benefits in the fixed matrix situation is by determining the value, in respect of each

individual network link, for all purposes, of:

$$\text{Link benefit} = Q_1 L_1 C_1 - Q_2 L_2 C_2$$

where $Q_1 Q_2$ = link flows before and after (i.e. Do-something e.f. DN)

$L_1 L_2$ = link lengths before and after (usually identical)

$C_1 C_2$ = link travel costs before and after.

It is, of course, essential that link benefits are then summed over the whole network of traffic-significant roads.

The traffic-management-based option recommended earlier in this chapter is less amenable to prior evaluation, particularly on economic grounds. It is therefore often assessed by on-the-spot before-and-after studies, on the basis of which the schemes can be adjusted to increase the benefits.

SUMMARY

a) For the smaller town, it is even more important than with the large town, to select the type of study appropriate to the specific problem – remembering that the objective is to produce a good transport plan, and not necessarily to do a sophisticated study.

b) The bypass solution is worthy of consideration in the smaller town, but it should of course be assessed in comparison with other possibilities including traffic management or an inner relief road.

c) The small town is less able to adopt the improved-public-transport, restrained-private-car use (carrot and stick) approach, but should always aim at optimum use of existing transport facilities.

d) Available small-town study approaches are basically a simpler transportation study or a form of fixed matrix growth factor exercise – the choice dependent on opportunities for land use or modal split change.

e) Alternative options for small towns should be developed and appraised by similar methods to those for larger towns.

11

The County as a Whole

We have already mentioned, in Chapter 2, how the components of an overall county transport strategy are separated out for detailed investigation. In the ensuing chapters these components, particularly in relation to the more pressing urban problems, have been examined in some detail and investigation techniques explored. It is now appropriate to revert to the overall county and consider how these segregated components can be brought together again. Before that however, it is necessary to expand somewhat on the techniques of county highway appraisal which were briefly described in Chapter 2.

The Case against a Synthetic County Model

The basic logic of adopting a manually-adjusted growth-factor approach to inter-urban traffic prediction has been explained. The alternative, frequently canvassed, is a transportation study based, to a large extent, on the approach already described for urban studies. And the county-wide model appears at first sight to offer many advantages — it looks at the whole county at one time, it can integrate the urban areas with the inter-urban investigation and can look at the modal split on a common basis throughout the county. The attractions of a county model however do not always bear close investigation — at least in respect of a significantly rural type of county — although for a county comprising a large proportion of minimally disjoint urban areas such as a loose conurbation or an urbanized sprawl, there may well be merit.

In the rural type county — for instance with a few quite large towns or cities but surrounded mainly by country interspersed with villages — an enlarged-urban type of county model is almost always inappropriate. The zoning system needed for the county as a whole would, for computer-space economy need to be relatively coarse. Inevitably then, the problems of zonal trip-end prediction from a household basis become greater. The applicability of externally-derived standard trip rates relating to urban areas is in any case highly debatable. This could clearly be solved by large surveys to derive study-specific trip rates, but this of course increases the cost of the county study very considerably. The larger zones also increase the importance of intra-zonal trips, thereby precluding their being virtually ignored, as is the practice in urban-area studies. Furthermore, the larger zones mean an increased likelihood that most schemes under investigation will be contained within only one or two zones — with similarly restricted impact.

A further argument against the adoption of a sophisticated county model on urban-study lines is the considerably more limited room for planning manoeuvre. Provisions for national scale inter-urban movement will undoubtedly be determined (largely if not entirely) at national level, becoming 'fixes' in the average county context. Other than those, given the existing road network, few *significant* changes are likely. Virtually the only logical argument in favour of sophisticated modelling techniques for the county inter-urban highway network is in order to integrate public transport movements. But the opportunities for modal choice in inter-urban movement are considerably less than in the towns – the flexibility of the car for inter-urban movement being of overwhelming importance – and the use of a two-mode model is therefore seldom justified.

For the relatively few rural-biased locations where a conventional transportation study is considered appropriate, possibly on a 'spider' network basis (i.e. using a very restricted number of roads to form the network, sufficing only to link zones without necessarily reflecting all route movements) the COMPACT 2 program described in the previous chapter may be suitable. For loose conurbations and sometimes for the more urban-sprawl type of county, a specially designed study would be more appropriate.

The Assessment of Need

So – in most rural-plus-town type counties, a transportation study leading to a county model is inappropriate and the manually-adjusted growth-factor exercise based on observed road and passenger traffic flows will often suffice. And the result of the growth-factor exercise (or of a modelling process where this was considered to be appropriate) would be design-year traffic flows on the existing road network, on which basis the Assessment-of-Need could be made. The manual adjustment would take account of such matters as future motorways, predictable major land-use changes (expanding ports, new hypermarkets, etc.) and increasing leisure attractions etc., which the conventional modelling process would take care of, without further adjustment.

Mentioned earlier and described more fully in the author's *Highway Planning Techniques*, one possible method for determining needy locations is, having divided up the county road network into reasonably homogenous sections, to determine the TAL (Travel and Accident Loss) for each section. This involves the concurrent measurement of speed and traffic flow along each section under present conditions and from these observations, by the application of standard inter-urban speed/flow relationships, predicting design year traffic speeds on each link.

Adopting standardized average road-user costs dependent on average speeds, the total annual travel cost in the design year of traffic using the present road is compared with the cost of the same traffic travelling at 70 km/h on a notional dual-carriageway road, the difference being the standardized travel loss. At the same time, the total annual accident loss is determined by application of typical pi accident rates and a standardized accident cost. Thus

> pi = personal injury

$$\text{TAL/km} = \text{£}QM(C_e - C_n) + 1\cdot56(A_e - A_n)$$

where Q = traffic flow in thousands of vehicles (at design year)

M = a multiplier to convert the traffic flow to an annual figure

C_e, C_n = £ travel cost per 1000 vehicle-km under existing and notional
        conditions

A_e, A_n = pi accident rate per 10^6 vehicle-km under existing and
        notional conditions.

Clearly, the road sections with the highest TAL values are those causing
the greatest economic loss to the community and therefore — on these
grounds at least — those most likely to be in need of improvement.

Development of Alternatives

Resulting from this exercise will be a list of ranked road sections from
those most in (economic) need of improvement down to those fully
adequate or even over-designed. It will not indicate solutions — merely
problem areas. At this stage, allowance should also be made for possible
improvements needed on environmental grounds, initially applying a
subjective weighting to their TAL ranking. From a rough cost per
kilometre for new road it is then possible to derive a broadly ranked
list of problem areas amounting to the available inter-urban budget
plus, say 50 per cent, the object being to reduce the number of schemes
for investigation down to manageable proportions. It is then necessary
to develop alternative solutions for the problem sections under
consideration.

Clearly, if several needy sections are contained in a single stretch of
road, a comprehensive treatment is desirable, possibly incorporating less
needy sections on grounds of continuity. This treatment might consist
of widening or dualling the existing road, of bypassing individual villages
or towns, or, and this should not be overlooked, the possibility of
relief by improving, or even providing, another road altogether.
Individual sections in need of improvement, that in fact represent travel
delays through minor urban areas, need careful consideration to ascertain
whether or not the problem is largely an inter-urban one or a local
urban one. If the problem is judged to be of an inter-urban nature, then
alternative lines for bypasses can be investigated, alongside the inevitable
existing-road-improvement option.

As mentioned in Chapter 2, the partial consideration of alternative
solutions can often initially be made on the basis of more detailed
estimates and a single-year assessment, dependent on the size of the
scheme; larger schemes warranting the NPV (net present value) approach
of the Department of the Environment's COBA method from the outset.
All but the smallest schemes should, before acceptance, be appraised by
some form of NPV assessment. If appropriate, schemes can be assessed
on a discounted cash-flow basis to determine their NPV by a manual
process, using key-year flows etc. as described in *Highway Planning
Techniques*. It must be remembered that economic considerations are
merely part of the justification for a road scheme, environmental
considerations particularly must also be assessed, albeit perhaps
subjectively. The overall object of the option-assessment exercise is
two-fold:

a) to reduce the number of schemes to a ranked list within, say ten per
cent of likely available funds, and

b) to determine the 'worthwhileness' (value for money) of the schemes
in that list.

A further benefit from the NPV assessment of all schemes is that it affords the basis for determining a phased programme, by indicating at least the economic advantages of deferring or expediting implementation of schemes. The importance of this consideration will be considered in the next chapter.

Overall Consistency

Apart from the economic and environmental justifications for road schemes, there is a possibility that certain, usually small, schemes may be necessary in order to permit the implementation of other aspects of a county or sub-regional transport policy. Examples of such considerations might be the improvement of access routes to a lorry park or to a new motorway, or the provision of purely holiday facilities.

This question of integration of policies in fact raises considerable problems. It is clearly essential that, for example, inter-urban schemes accepted for incorporation in the overall plan should not conflict with, or impose unforeseen problems on, adjacent urban proposals. An example of this, in extremis, might be to terminate a major new motorway at the outskirts of an urban area without providing means for dissipating the traffic throughout the urban network. And this sort of county-wide consistency checking can be done reasonably easily — the prime requisite is a clear view of the overall picture. It is also desirable that improvements, policies etc. adopted by one county are at least compatible with those of neighbouring counties — for example, a dual carriageway inter-urban road changing at the county boundary to a single carriageway road is (probably) to be avoided.

Inter-disciplinary Choice

The more difficult aspect of county-wide integration is the problem of deciding for example between an urban bus subsidy and an inter-urban village bypass. Over a plan period these two examples might cost comparable sums, the subsidy being say 15 years at a small amount, the bypass being a lump-sum payment in an intermediate year. The urban subsidy might be a possibly marginal part of an urban package which was assessed as a whole — on a design-year all-traveller consumer-surplus rate of return. The village bypass would have been appraised in isolation and assessed in terms of road-user costs by determination of NPV/cost or possibly a single-year rate of return. The evaluation criteria are in no significant way comparable. Different items are considered by different processes. This is understandable, and in the circumstances, correct. The choice, if choice there must be, between the two possible ways of spending the available money must be a political one.

One possible means of providing some assistance to the politicians in the task of such inter-disciplinary, inter-area choices is by an extension of the accessibility contour technique described in Chapter 9 on Urban Option Assessment. A whole-county map could be prepared, indicating all locations in the county from which some part of the jobs in the county are within, say, 30 minutes travel time by public transport and/or, say, 20 minutes by private car. Such a map could be developed from information on numbers of jobs within the specified time-period from each zone. Similar maps could be prepared for accessibility to other trip attractors — shopping centres, leisure facilities, etc. There still remains the question of weighting work accessibilities against, say, shopping accessibility, but at least this is a more readily understandable concept.

And the end result of the final overall county-wide assessment and integration is a package of schemes and policies for a roughly 15-year period, within a hopefully realistic, overall financial constraint. In the next chapter the problems of converting the package into a programme will be considered.

SUMMARY

a) In most counties, other than loose conurbations or urban sprawls, a conventional urban-type transportation study is not appropriate for county-wide, inter-urban appraisal. Manually adjusted growth-factoring will usually suffice.

b) Inter-urban road-scheme problem areas can be located by an Assessment-of-Need exercise using techniques such as the TAL method.

c) Alternative solutions for each problem area should be postulated and assessed, eventually using some form of net present-value economic technique.

d) It is essential that policies preferred for one sectoral or disciplinary aspect of a county transport plan are compatible and consistent with the whole, and other parts of the plan, and, as far as possible, with those of neighbouring areas.

e) The necessarily subjective (political) balancing of, for example, urban and rural needs, which may well be inter-disciplinary, can to some extent be assisted by such measures as work- or leisure-accessibility. These only make the problem more readily understood — there is still a subjective decision to be made.

12

The Development of
an Implementation Programme

So far, by the application of the various processes described in previous chapters, we have suggested how an overall county-wide transport system, or plan, might be developed for a notional 15-year period. This preferred overall plan will have been built up of policies and plans for expenditure on public-transport support, parking provision and the use of both existing and new roads — all within a notional financial planning budget. Three particularly important points relating to the end product of this planning process need to be emphasized:

a) the plan is for the whole planning period — not just the first year or few years,

b) the plan is not based on a guarantee of financing, but on the predicted total financial availability over the planning period,

c) the plan is an integrated package of several inter-dependent components.

The Constraints

Considering firstly the matter of finance availability, it must be realised that expenditure on transport matters derives very largely from public funds. And public funds are largely collected on an annual basis from the public in the form of local rates or national taxes. Very large blocks of funds are therefore not immediately available other than from loans — which in turn of course demand annual servicing. Clearly central government is more able to even out fluctuations in demands for finance than are local government bodies, but this is merely a question of degree, the principle still applies. For this financial reason, even if for no other reason, it is preferable to spread the implementation of a transport plan more-or-less evenly through the plan period.

The financial reason for developing a time-stream for plan implementation is, however, amply reinforced both by the available-capacity restraints on implementation and by the non-immediacy of the demand. Inasmuch as most urban-road schemes are designed in local authority drawing offices, the pace of implementation is to some extent governed by the capacity of the design office. Similarly, construction capacity and supervisory staff availability are also limited, although once again, this is largely a question of degree. Balancing out this 'spendability' restraint, though, is the fact that the demand for improved transport facilities is a growing one from base-year to design-year. There is not therefore an immediate need for design-year level facilities.

Acknowledging then the financial necessities and/or the merits of spreading the implementation of the overall transport plan over the plan period, there are other constraints upon the programming process. One of the more important constraints is obviously that of already started schemes and policies. The actual construction of roads, carparks or public transport interchanges inevitably takes more than a single year. Any scheme started in one year imposes an inevitable and usually inescapable commitment to expenditure in the next one or more years, and these commitments must have a prior claim on available resources.

Similarly, but perhaps somewhat less obviously, an ongoing annual commitment to, for instance, public transport revenue support (subsidy) cannot be stopped at the stroke of a pen. This expenditure too has therefore a prior claim on available annual resources.

Further considerations of completely different natures but nonetheless greatly affecting the programming process are the availability of land and the need for integrated yet phased implementation. Even if funds are available and designs completed, the construction of a new carpark or an urban highway may easily be delayed awaiting completion of land acquisition processes. And indeed, a scheme for which land is immediately available might well warrant construction earlier than strictly justifiable. At all stages in the programming process however it is essential to ensure that the comprehensivity of the transport strategy is maintained. For example, to build all the new roads included in a transport plan before carrying out any of the moves to improve public transport facilities would be as much out of balance as to initiate a park-and-ride parking facility without the bus service.

Five-Year Blocks

In order to meet many of the requirements mentioned above it is best initially to divide up the list of schemes and policies in the overall plan into blocks of, say, 5 years. We have already seen, in Chapter 2, how these blocks — years 0 to 5, 5 to 10, and 10 to 15 — break down into, very broadly, commitments; new proposals likely to be implemented; and longer term new proposals which will probably be subject to later revision. Clearly there is need to ensure, as far as possible, that the most advantageous schemes and policies are implemented first, with less necessary proposals left till later. To some extent this advantage ranking can be done subjectively; for instance, virtually all traffic-management measures, if worth doing at all, will afford very considerable benefits at low cost. At the same time, correct ranking of low-cost schemes and policies is obviously of less importance than that of more expensive proposals.

There is merit therefore in carrying out some form of secondary appraisal of the more expensive proposals incorporated in a preferred overall strategy. This need not necessarily be to confirm their individual worth (although this is sometimes in question) but rather to ascertain an appropriate date for their implementation. Depending on the size or scale of the proposal being investigated, the secondary appraisal could include economic assessment ranging from a simple, single-year rate-of-return determination to a more sophisticated, discounted-cash-flow type of net present-value determination. Going somewhat further than just the assessment of an individual proposal, it is often worthwhile to investigate the phasing of the whole plan in respect of alternative phasings of blocks of schemes and policies. This would inevitably entail a series of net present-value calculations based on interpolated 5-year intervals within the plan period and possible extrapolating on some standardized basis for up to 15 years thereafter.

The First Five Years

Having ascertained the apparently most appropriate five-year periods for the implementation of individual proposals within the overall plan it is useful — indeed necessary — to programme at least the first five-year block by specific years. As mentioned above, account must be taken of existing financial commitments and total annual resources available. It is also important that, at least in the immediate five-year period, the estimates are realistic both in terms of the total cost of an individual proposal and also in terms of realistic implementation time. It is just as important from a financial viewpoint to guard against underspending as it is to keep within the provision.

In a notional county, planning the spending of £75 million over a 15-year period on all relevant transport matters (exclusive of maintenance, which is assumed to be substantially fixed) would indicate annual expenditure of the order of £5 million — in present-year values. The present commitments stretching through the 0- to 5-year period could well total nearly half of this sum, with residual resources 'available' in Year 1 only about ten per cent of the apparent total. This commitment aspect is illustrated by the following notional figures, which for simplicity, indicate a few expensive proposals rather than the more likely large number of less expensive proposals:

(All figures in £ million)

Year	Road A	Road B	PT Subsidy	Road C	Road D	Carpark etc	Road E	Total	Residue
Earlier years				2			1½	(NA)	(NA)
-1	2		½	1			1½	5	0
0	2	1	½	1	½			5	0
1	1	1	½	1	1			4½	½
2		1	½		½	1		3	2
3			½			1½		2	3
4			¾					¾	4¼
5			¾					¾	4¼
Totals years 1-5 incl.	1	2	3	1	1½	2½	0	11	14

Implementation lead-time

In allotting proposals to specific years in the first five-year block it is important to bear in mind the lead-time involved in, at least, highway scheme implementation. It is not uncommon for the design, statutory and contractual processes required before a single spit of earth is moved to take 3 to 5 years. Unless therefore, the design of a road scheme has been commissioned — as a stock task — before a preferred strategy is determined, there is little chance, certainly with major schemes, of implementation in the first five-year block.

Because comprehensive transport planning is a continuous, non-static process, the proposals mooted for the third five-year block are unlikely to be implemented without a second, strategic level, appraisal. It is the middle, second five-year block of proposals that are of the greatest significance in each cycle of the planning process. And it is important always to bear in mind the future financial effect of present-day measures. The relatively cheap (capital-cost) initiation of, say, a segregated-way bus service may well impose a long-term commitment to revenue support.

Monitoring

Finally, the optimal programming of proposals derived from a comprehensive transport appraisal can never alone be an entirely adequate means of financial and administrative control. There must also be some form of monitoring — the comparison of plans with achievements. On a financial level it is of course a continuing and practicable necessity to compare actual with planned expenditure — if for no other reason than to inject realism into future annual expenditure estimating.

On a physical level however, other than by comparing completion percentages with planned progress the monitoring process is less simple. What is really wanted is a measure of the effects produced by the comprehensive measures as they are implemented. These sorts of effects, however, are relatively slow to be perceived. Any monitoring of effects must therefore almost inevitably be a long-term process, to some extent founded on behavioural, environmental, and social surveys, such as are required for urban transportation studies. Other than these objective measures, some degree of monitoring can be achieved by mere observation on the ground. This should be done as much as possible, but its subjectivity must be allowed for in assessing the results.

Some form of assessment of achievements is essential — for there are many subjective and/or political decisions in the continuous comprehensive transport planning process. We may aim for perfect solutions — all we are likely to achieve are workable compromises, robust enough to accommodate the inevitable future changes.

SUMMARY

a) It is important that a phased programme of implementation is prepared — if for no other reason, to ensure that the preferred -strategy is implemented in a planned and integrated manner in line with available financial resources.

b) Initially, a 15-year plan should be divided into 5-year blocks or phases, the first of which will be largely dictated by existing commitments and those already planned.

c) While the proposals intended for implementation in the third 5-year block are likely to be re-assessed before they are actually put in hand, those in the second phase at least should be scrutinized more carefully on an individual scheme basis.

d) Because of the long lead-time of at least highway schemes, it is unlikely that any wholly new scheme can be implemented until the second 5-year phase.

e) Both financial and physical monitoring of achievements are essential parts of the comprehensive transport planning process — not least as a check on the many subjective decisions therein.

Appendix - Transport Planning Legislation in England and Wales

In the past, in England and Wales, the components of a comprehensive transport system have been subject to different levels of administrative control, different sources and levels of financing and a variety of legal backing. With the 1972 Local Government Act, however, the various levels of local government authority concerned with transport matters have been unified and absorbed into the new county structure. At the same time, under Sections 202 and 203, overall responsibility for the county-wide integration of public transport services was placed on each of the new counties, where previously only some conurbations (metropolitan counties) had held that responsibility.

In their December 1972 response to the comments of the House of Commons Expenditure Committee reporting on urban transport planning, the Government, in House of Commons Paper 57, Session 1972-73 (Cmnd 5366), gave one of the first public intimations that the whole system of transport financing in England and Wales was to be changed. The objectives of the proposed new grant system were stated to be 'to promote the development and implementation of comprehensive transport policies' and 'to give local authorities greater freedom from detailed central government control'.

This Government statement was followed in August 1973 by an administrative notification, in the Department of the Environment's Circular 104/73 (Welsh Office Circular 193/73) of the proposal that, subject to Parliamentary approval of the necessary legislation, a new system of grants for local transport should come into effect for the financial year 1975/76. The new grant system is to replace:

a) principal road specific grants (75%) under Section 235 of the Highways Act, 1959,

b) public transport infrastructure grants (25-75%) under Section 56 of the Transport Act, 1968,

c) rural bus and ferry grants under Section 34 of the Transport Act, 1968,

d) contributions (50%) towards the cost of transportation studies.

The new legislation providing for the new, comprehensive, transport grant system is designed to eliminate any financial bias towards a particular form of expenditure, to encourage comprehensive transport planning at county level, to reduce central government involvement in individual proposals and, as far as possible, to distribute the available funds to accord with the various needs of different areas.

Particularly relevant recent British Government publications, at the
time of writing include:

DOE Circular 104/73 Local Transport Grants.

DOE Circular 27/74 Transport Supplementary Grant; More Details of
the New System.

DOE Circular 60/74 Transport Supplementary Grant; Submissions for
1975/76.

A Select Preferred Bibliography

Books

Berry, D.S., and others, *The Technology of Urban Transportation*, North Western University Press, 1963.

Brierley, J. *Parking of Motor Vehicles (2nd Edn.)*, Applied Science Pub. 1972.

Bruton, M.J. *Introduction to Transportation Planning*, Hutchinson Technical Education, 1970.

Buchanan Report, *Traffic in Towns*, HMSO, 1963.

Department of Architecture, Planning and Quantity Surveying, *Urban Public Transport*, Glenrothes Development Corporation, 1972.

Heggie, I.G. *Transport Engineering Economics*, McGraw-Hill, 1972.

Hobbs & Richardson, *Traffic Engineering Vols. 1 & 2*, Pergamon Press, 1967.

Lane, Powell, & Prestwood-Smith, *Analytical Transport Planning*, Duckworth, 1971.

Meyer, Kain, & Wohl, *The Urban Transportation Problem*, Harvard University Press, 1965.

Roth, G., *Paying for Roads*, Penguin, 1967.

Schumer, L.A., *The Elements of Transport*, Butterworths, 1968.

Sharp, C., *Problems of Urban Passenger Transport*, Leicester University Press, 1967.

Special Report 125, *Parking Principles*, Highway Research Board, 1971.

Traffic Assignment Manual, US Bureau of Public Roads, 1964.

Wells, G.R., *Traffic Engineering — an Introduction*, Griffin, 1970.

Wells, G.R., *Highway Planning Techniques*, Griffin, 1971.

T R R L Reports and other Publications

LR 200, Herrmann, P.G., *Forecasts of Vehicle Ownership in Counties and County Boroughs in Great Britain*, 1968.

LR 221, Ellson, P.B., *Parking — Dynamic capacity of car parks*, 1969

LR 288, Tulpule, A.H., *Forecasts of Vehicles and Traffic in Great Britain 1969*, and LR 543 for 1972 revision.

LR 289, Ellson, P.B. and others, *Parking — Effect of stall markings*, 1969.

LR 356, Blackmore, F.C., *Capacity of single-level Intersections*, 1970.

LR 396, Dawson, R.F.F., *Current Cost of Road Accidents in Great Britain*, 1971.

LR 422, Maycock, G., *Implementation of Traffic Restraint*, 1972.

LR 448, Webster, F.V., *Priority to Buses as part of Traffic Management*, 1972.

LR 521, Cundill & Watts, *Bus Boarding and Alighting Times*, 1973.

LR 566, Wigan & Bamford, *A Comparative Network Simulation of ... Traffic Restraint*, 1973.

LR 569, Holroyd & Robertson, *Strategies for Area Traffic Control systems — present and future*, 1973.

LR 570, Symposium proceedings, *Bus Priority*, 1973.

LR 576, Andrews, R.D., *A Survey of Bus Crew Scheduling Practices*, 1973.

TP 75, Dawson, R.F.F., *Economic Assessment of Road Improvement Schemes*, 1968.

—, Grant & Russell, *Opportunities in automated urban transport*, 1973.

Department of the Environment Publications

DOE/HMSO Publications

Urban Traffic Engineering Techniques, 1965.

Parking in Town Centres, Planning Bulletin No. 7, 1965.

Better Use of Town Roads, 1967.

Traffic Management & Parking, 1969.

Lorry Parking, Working Party Report, 1971.

Getting the Best Roads for our Money — the COBA Method of Appraisal, 1972.

Urban Transport Planning, House of Commons Paper 57, Session 1972/3, Cmnd 5366.

Bus Demonstration Projects — Summary Reports etc.

No. 1 *Bus Detection — Bus Priority at Traffic Control Signals*

No. 2 *Tottenham — Contra-flow Bus Lane within a One-way Traffic Scheme*

No. 3 *Reading — Bus Priority within a Comprehensive Traffic Management Scheme*

No. 4 *Manchester — Retention of Bus Access within a One-way Traffic Scheme*

Green Light for Buses

Studies of Rural Transport in Devon and West Suffolk, reports by Steering Groups, 1971.

MAU (Mathematical Advisory Unit) Notes

132 Wagon, D.J., *The SELNEC Model ... and the modelling process*, 1969.

179 McIntosh & Quarmby, *Generalised costs ... in Transport Planning*, 1970.

201 Mackinder and others, *COMPACT 2*

228 Down, D.W., *Standard definitions for Land Use/Transportation Studies*, 1971.

DOE Circulars etc.

Technical Memorandum H 7/71, *Junction Design (Interim)*
DOE Circular 57/73, *Lorries and the Environment*
DOE Circular 82/73, *Bus Operation in Residential and Industrial Areas*

Institution of Civil Engineers — Transportation Engineering Group Discussion Papers

Houghton-Evans, W., *Role of Engineer in Town Planning*, May, 1968.
Proudlove & Shaw, *Interaction of Transportation and LandUse Planning*, Apr. 1969.
Burns, Wilson, & Holland, *The South East Regional Plan*, Oct. 1970.
Rhodes & Wilson, *Planning and Transport Models for the South Hampshire plan*, Nov. 1970.
Lichfield, N., *Stevenage Public Transport*, Feb. 1971.
Dower & Maw, *Planning for Leisure Travel*, Oct. 1971.
Bridle, R.J., *Problems of Mathematical Modelling for Inter-regional Road Location*, May 1972.
Gwilliam, K.M., *Economics of Subsidised Transport*, May 1972.
Salter, R.J., *Transportation Requirements of Large Organisations*, Jan. 1973.
Kaukas, B., *Requirements, design and operation of Public Transport Interchange Terminals*, Feb. 1973.
Lane & Chu, *Pedestrian Problems*, March 1973.
Ferguson, J.A., *Area Traffic Control by Computer*, May 1973.

Articles in Traffic Engineering & Control — Printerhall : London

Wootton & Pick, *Travel Estimating from Census Data*, July 1967.
Lyons, D.J., *Bus Travel in Town Centres*, May 1969.
Marsh, R., *Ways of Promoting Public Transport*, May 1969.
Bridgood, R., *Who Pays for Parking*, June 1969.
Oxley, P.R., *Dial-a-Ride — demand actuated public transport*, July 1970.
Millard, R.S., *Roundabouts and Signals*, May 1971.
Bell, R.A., *Traffic, Parking and Regional Shopping Centres*, Sept. 1971.
Choudbury, A.R., *Park-and-Ride as a Modal Choice*, Oct. 1971.
Good, G.E., *A gravity distribution model*, Dec. 1971 — Jan. 1972.
Brierley, J., *Whither Parking?*, March/April 1972.
Huddart, K.W., and others, *Bus Priority in Greater London*, Nov. 1972 — Apr. 1973.

Other Publications

Public Transport

Buckles, P.A., *Stevenage Superbus Experiment*, Paper to University of Newcastle-upon-Tyne Fourth Annual Symposium 'Promoting Public Transport', April 1973.
Leopold, H., *Marketing of Public Transport — an Instrument of Traffic Policy*, Paper to Manchester University Sixth Symposium on Future of Conurbation Transportation, October 1972.
Skerry, P., *Bus Services with Knobs on*, Coaching Journal, March 1973.

Goodwin, P.B., *Effects of Free Public Transport,* Transport Planning and Technology 1973, Vol. 1, pp. 159—174.

Traffic Management

Duff, J.D., *Engineering for Road Safety,* Public Works and Municipal Services Congress, November 1970.

Binks, R.K., *Pedestrian Precincts,* Institution of Municipal Engineers, 1973.

Parking

O'Flaherty, C., *This Parking Business,* Jnl. of Institution of Municipal Engineers, December 1968.

Making Parking Pay, Report of British Parking Association Seminar, 1972.

Car Parking, PTRC Seminar Report, 1971.

Glanville, J., *Physical Design of Car Parks,* Municipal and Public Services Journal, 9 Feb. 1973.

Parking — an Insight Investigation, Sunday Times, 5 April 1970.

Dore, E., *Cost of Multi-storey Car Parks,* Surveyor, 22 Oct. 1971.

Smith, E., *Parking Restraint by Pricing,* Surveyor, 6 Aug. 1971.

Bruton, M.J., *Parking Policy as an Instrument of Traffic Restraint,* The Highway Engineer, January 1973.

Routh, D.T., *Parking and Traffic Restraint,* Traffex Seminar, October 1973.

Transportation Studies

Wootton & Pick, *A Model for Trips Generated by Households,* Journal of Transport Economic Policy Vol. 1, pp. 137—153, 1967.

Burrell, J.E., *Multiple Route Assignment and its application to Capacity Restraint,* 4th International Symposium on Traffic Flow, Karlsruhe, 1968.

Tressider, J.O., and others, *The London Transportation Study — Methods & Techniques,* Proceedings of Institution of Civil Engineers, March, 1968.

McIntosh & Martin, *Use of Computers in Transportation Planning,* Journal of Institution of Highway Engineers, August 1968.

Lamb, G.M., *Transportation Studies and Policy Making,* Journal of Institution of Municipal Engineers, July 1970.

Warner, B.T., *Moving Goods in Urban Areas,* Chartered Institution of Transport Journal, September 1973.

Lassiere, A., *Environmental Evaluation of Transport Plans at the Strategy Level,* PTRC Conference, June 1973.

Index